100 WALKS IN YORKSHIRE

NORTH YORK MOORS AND WOLDS

GARY RICHARDSON

First published in 2018 by
The Crowood Press Ltd
Ramsbury, Marlborough
Wiltshire SN8 2HR

www.crowood.com

British Library Cataloguing-in-Publication Data
A catalogue record for this book is available from the British Library.

ISBN 978 1 78500 385 1

Front cover: Shutterstock

Mapping in this book is sourced from the following products: OS Explorer OL26, OL27, 229,
290, 294, 295, 300, 301, 302

Every effort has been made to ensure the accuracy of this book. However, changes can occur
during the lifetime of an edition. The Publishers cannot be held responsible for any errors or
omissions or for the consequences of any reliance on the information given in this book, but
should be very grateful if walkers could let us know of any inaccuracies by writing to us at
the address above or via the website.

As with any outdoor activity, accidents and injury can occur. We strongly advise readers to
check the local weather forecast before setting out and to take an OS map. The Publishers
accept no responsibility for any injuries which may occur in relation to following the walk
descriptions contained within this book.

Typeset by Jean Cussons Typesetting, Diss, Norfolk
Printed and bound in India by Replika Press Pvt Ltd

Contents

How to Use this Book

The walks in the book are ordered regionally, and then by distance within each region, starting with the shortest and ending with the longest. An information panel for each walk shows the distance, start point (see below), a summary of level of difficulty (easy/moderate/difficult/strenuous), OS map(s) required, and suggested pubs/cafés at the start/end of the walk or on the way. An introductory sentence at the beginning of each walk briefly describes the route and terrain.

Readers should be aware that starting point postcodes have been supplied for satnav purposes and are not indicative of exact locations. Some start points are so remote that there is no postcode.

MAPS

There are ninety-one maps covering the 100 walks. Some of the walks are extensions of existing routes and the information panel for these walks will tell you the distance of the short and long versions of the walk, depending on whether you wish to combine two walks or tackle each singly.

The routes marked on the maps are punctuated by a series of numbered waypoints. These relate to the same numbers shown in the walk description.

Start Points

The start of each walk is given as a postcode and also a six-figure grid reference number prefixed by two letters (which indicates the relevant square on the National Grid). More information on grid references is found on Ordnance Survey maps.

Parking

Many of the car parks suggested are public, but for some walks you will have to park on the roadside or in a lay-by. Please be considerate when leaving your car and do not block access roads or gates. Also, if parking in a pub car park for the duration of the walk, please try to avoid busy times.

COUNTRYSIDE CODE

- Consider the local community and other people enjoying the outdoors
- Leave gates and property as you find them and follow paths
- Leave no trace of your visit and take litter home
- Keep dogs under effective control
- Plan ahead and be prepared
- Follow advice and local signs

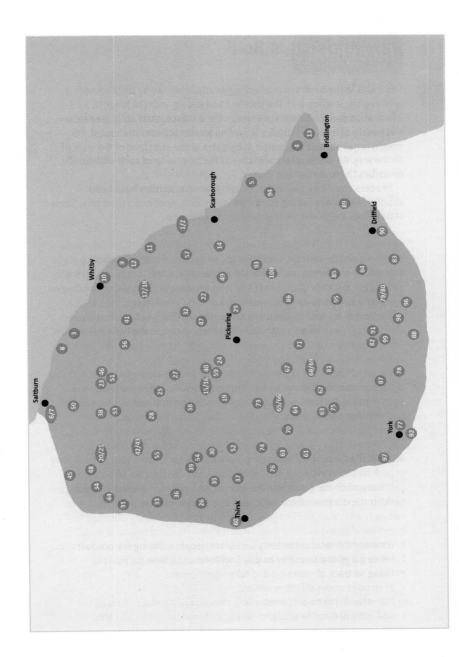

Bridlington
13
4
Scarborough
5
94
Driffield
89
90
1/2
14
83
11
57
93
100
85
84
Whitby
9
49
95
10
12
17/18
22
86
32
79/80
96
41
47
29
98
Pickering
99
88
3
56
71
82 91
8
82
99
46
40 24
68/69
81
87
23
51
27
59
78
25
15/16
19
67
Saltburn
50
38
53
28
58
73
65/66
64
63
75
6/7
70
62
97
York
77
42/43
30
52
74
92
20/21
55
39 54
61
48
35
37
76
63
45
34
36
26
44
31
33
60 Thirsk

Cloughton

START At TA019951, Cloughton Wyke, YO13 0BB

DISTANCE 3¾ miles (6.0 km) or 6¾ miles (10.8 km)

PARKING Roadside parking at the end of Salt Pans Road

MAPS Explorer OL27; OS Sheets Landranger 101

WHERE TO EAT AND DRINK Hayburn Wyke Inn www.hayburnwykeinn.co.uk

Two beautiful walks along the cliff tops, linked by a section of disused railway line. These are mainly along cliff top paths and disused railway lines, which can be muddy in places.

1 From the parking area go left down some steps to join the Cleveland Way, which is followed along the cliff tops towards Hayburn Wyke. It's generally easy walking, apart from the steep section of steps through the woods near to Sycarham Farm, to reach the woodlands at Hayburn Wyke.

2 Enter the woods and descend wooden steps. At the path junction, keep right along the Cleveland Way. The path continues to descend through the woods, with glimpses of the rocky cove below, to reach another path junction above a stream. A short diversion to the rocky cove is possible by going right over the footbridge at this point, otherwise go left uphill along the path through the woods.

3 Keep straight ahead at the cross paths, up steps to reach a gate. Go through the gate and diagonally left across the field, exit via a gate onto a road. Pass the Hayburn Wyke Inn and keep along the road to reach the disused railway line. Go left along this and follow it back to a stone bridge over the line. Go up the steps to the right onto Salt Pans Road, go left over the bridge and follow the lane back to the parking area.

4 For the longer walk, keep along the old railway line to reach a road, exit through a gate and go right along the road, then left,

passing the Station Tearooms, to regain the old railway line, and continue as far as the bridge over Field Lane.

5 Go right down the steps and then right under the bridge and follow the lane to its end edge of the cliffs above Flat Scar. Join the Cleveland Way again and go left along the cliff top path, which is followed back to the parking area.

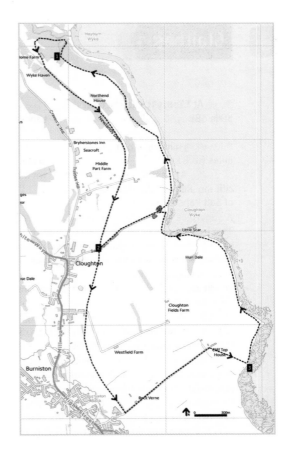

Hayburn Wyke – A beautiful woodland area owned by the National Trust, which reaches down to a magnificent rocky cove complete with a tumbling waterfall and giant boulders.

Staithes

START At NZ781185, Staithes car park, TS13 5AD

MAPS Explorer OL27; OS Sheets Landranger 94

DISTANCE 4 miles (6.5 km)

WHERE TO EAT AND DRINK Various places in Staithes

SUMMARY An easy walk mainly along cliff top and woodland paths

A superb exploration of Captain Cook country.

[1] From Staithes car park, go right down Staithes Lane towards the harbour, just beyond the Cod and Lobster. Turn right, up Church Street, passing Captain Cook's Cottage. At the top of the street, climb steps and go left at the Cleveland Way marker. Go up more steps and pass a farm on your right.

[2] Continue over fields to reach the tops of the cliffs, go right along the fenced path, climbing towards Beacon Hill. At the top of the climb, the views back towards Staithes reveal Boulby Cliffs, at 679 feet high, they are some of the highest in England. Continue along the cliff top path to reach the hamlet of Port Mulgrave.

[3] Go right along Rosedale Lane, keep on to a T-junction in front of the church. Go left to reach the A174 road. Carefully cross this and go straight ahead into Porret Lane. Follow this through the houses until it joins Back Lane. Go right along the lane, where it turns sharp left and leave it by going straight ahead into a field, down to a footbridge over Dales Beck. Cross this and take the path on the right alongside the beck. Follow this as it climbs through the woods, passing scrub land, before dropping down to another bridge over the beck.

[4] Re-cross the beck and climb up towards Seaton Hall, pass to the right of this and follow the farm track to reach the A174 again. Go left along this and then right into Staithes Lane, which is followed back to the car park.

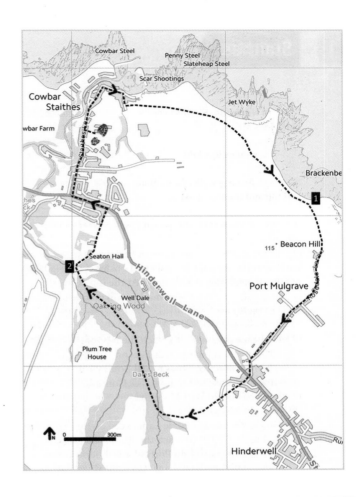

Points of interest

Captain Cook's Cottage – Here, there is a Heritage Trail Plaque which reads:
'The young James Cook received his taste of the sea and ships in
this harbour village, where he worked as an assistant to William
Sanderson, merchant, for eighteen months, from 1745.'

Bempton

START At TA197738, RSPB Bempton Cliffs car park, YO15 1JF

PARKING Visitor Centre car park

DISTANCE 4 miles (6.5 km)

MAPS Explorer 301; OS Sheets Landranger 101

SUMMARY An easy walk mainly along cliff top and country lanes

WHERE TO EAT AND DRINK RSPB Visitor Centre

An interesting walk along cliff top and country lanes with excellent opportunities for bird spotting.

① From the car park walk along Cliff Lane towards Bempton village to reach the B1229.

② Go right past the White House pub, and through the village. Keep on along the B1229 at the end of the houses to reach the village of Buckton. Keep following the road through the village.

③ Just after passing Buckton Gate, on your left, you will come to a footpath signpost next to the village pond. Leave the road here by going right onto Hoddy Cows Lane which is followed along the edges of fields for about 1½ miles to reach the cliff top path at Buckton cliffs.

④ Go right along the cliff top path and follow it back towards the car park. After about a mile, go right along the path back to the RSPB Visitor Centre and car park. It is possible to extend the walk along the cliff top paths if desired.

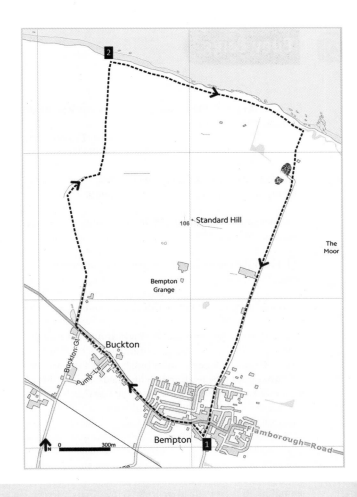

Points of interest

RSPB Reserve – The Bempton Cliffs reserve is probably one of the finest on the British mainland; its 400 feet high cliffs provide nesting sites for thousands of gannets, kittiwakes, razorbills, guillemots and puffins. There is constant noise and smell! The birds provide an extremely spectacular flying display below you.

5 Filey Brigg

START At TA123816, Filey Country Park car park, YO14 9ET

DISTANCE 4¼ miles (6.8 km)

SUMMARY An easy walk mainly along cliff top and field paths

PARKING Pay and display car park

MAPS Explorer 301; OS Sheets Landranger 101

WHERE TO EAT AND DRINK Various places in Filey

A walk around Filey along cliff top and field paths with extensive sea views across the bay.

① From the car park, take the path through the woods of Horn Dale. At the bottom go right up the winding path onto the cliff tops. Keep along the cliff path to descend steps to Ravine Road, keep left onto Beach Road and follow this to the junction with Car Gate Hill.

② Turn right here into Station Road and go right to the T-junction, where you need to go left, then immediately right onto Scarborough Road, the A1039. Keep going along this until the houses stop. Here, go right onto a lane leading to Filey Fields. Follow this along the field edges to reach the cliff tops above Fox Castle.

③ Join the Cleveland Way here and go right along the cliff top path, over North Cliff to reach ponds at the start of Filey Brigg.

④ Follow the path out onto Filey Brigg to Carr Nase, where there are wonderful views across the bay towards towering white cliffs at Bempton. Retrace your route back to the ponds, then go left along the cliff tops. A winding path leads down into Horn Dale. At the bottom. Go right uphill through the woods back to the car park.

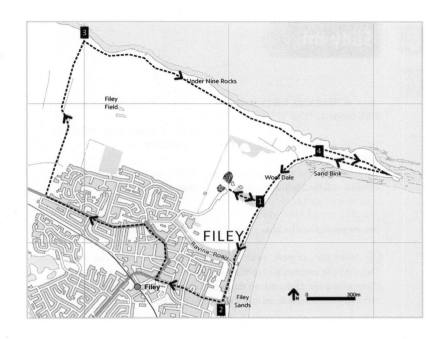

Points of interest

Filey Brigg – The rocky promontory of Filey Brigg, heavily capped with glacial clays, is a haven for both geologists and ornithologists. The fossiliferous limestones and grits dip at a steep angle under the Brigg, giving the north and south sides a very different appearance. Protruding eastwards into the North Sea, the Brigg is an ideal place for watching passing seabirds and waders while the adjacent cliff top fields and ponds provide a differing habitat for other species.

Saltburn

START At NZ668215, Cat Nab car park in Saltburn, TS12 1N

DISTANCE 4½ miles (7.2 km) or 8¼ miles (13.3 km)

SUMMARY Moderate walks along cliff top and field paths

PARKING Pay and display car park

MAPS Explorer OL27; OS Sheets Landranger 101

WHERE TO EAT AND DRINK Various places in Saltburn

Two beautiful walks along the cliff tops and field paths.

① From the car park, go left in front of the toilets onto the coast road, then right along this to the Ship Inn. Just behind this, go along the Cleveland Way, up steps, climbing up on to Huntcliff. Keep along the cliff top path to reach an abandoned building.

② Leave the Cleveland Way and go right over a stile and the field beyond, to cross the railway line. Keep ahead across the next field, cross over a stile, keep heading for Warsett Hill until a rough track is reached. Go right along this, which contours around the hill to a stile beside the railway line. Re-cross the tracks and follow the path downhill alongside fields to a track beside Brough House Farm.

③ Keep on downhill. Bear left at houses to emerge beside the Ship Inn again. Go left along the road back to the car park.

④ For the longer walk, keep on along cliff tops following the Cleveland Way to reach the village of Skinningrove.

⑤ Go right along the road between houses. After crossing the river for the second time, go right uphill on a footpath through trees to reach the A174 opposite Carlin How. Cross the main road into Carlin How, pass the village chippy onto Muriel Street. At the end, take the lane Back Street across fields. This is part of the Cleveland Street walk between Guisborough and Loftus. Keep on uphill. At the top cross the road, then downhill through more fields to a path junction just before trees.

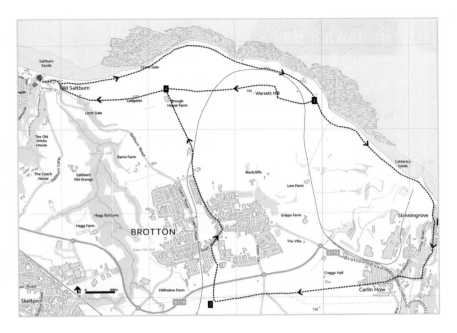

[6] Go right here to cross the A174 via a footbridge, then along a wooded path to exit onto a road beside the hospital. Go straight ahead along Child Street. Bear right along High Street, taking the second left, Saltburn Road. Follow this to where it turns sharp left. Leave the road and take the track between houses. Cross the railway line, go through the farm yard and then across fields to reach Brough House Farm.

Points of interest

Skinningrove – The village had an agricultural and fishing economy until the opening of local ironstone workings in 1848 initiated an industrialization boom. A railway was built by 1865, and iron smelting began in 1874. A jetty on the coast built in 1880 allowed seagoing vessels to carry heavy cargoes from the area. Mining continued until 1958 and primary iron production until the 1970s.

Runswick Bay

START At NZ809159, Runswick Bay car park, TS13 3HT

DISTANCE 5 miles (8 km)

SUMMARY An easy walk mainly along disused railway lines and coastal paths

PARKING Pay and display car park

MAPS Explorer OL27; OS Sheets Landranger 94

WHERE TO EAT AND DRINK The Runswick Bay Hotel www.therunswickbay.co.uk

A walk mainly along disused railway lines with good views from the coastal paths.

1 From the car park, go left uphill following the road to the junction opposite the Runswick Bay Hotel. Here, go left along Ellerby Lane, passing houses on the right and keep on until a dip in the road.

2 Leave the road by going left up a steep muddy path onto the disused railway track. At first this is quite overgrown with trees/ bushes but soon opens out and provides easy walking. Keep on for approximately 2 miles until a gate is reached close to the cliff tops. (At the time of writing, the permissive path along the railway track was closed from this point. If it is open at the time of walking, continue along until the road is reached, go left and follow this to its end in Kettleness.)

3 Leave the railway by going through the gate on the left to join the Cleveland Way. Go right along the cliff top path through fields to reach Kettleness village, with fine views along the coast.

4 Retrace the outward route along the cliff tops then keep on along the Cleveland Way, heading back towards Runswick Bay. At High Cliff a steep descent down wood fronted steps begins, these can be wet and muddy in places.

5 Towards the bottom at Hob Holes, Calais Beck has to be crossed. The bridge was missing at the time of writing and the crossing could

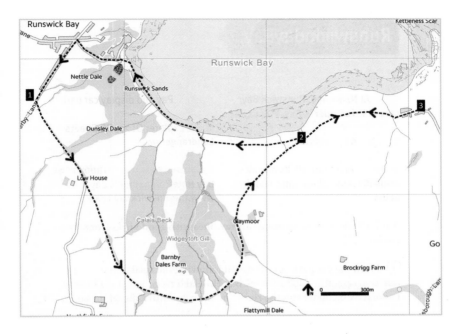

be awkward if the beck was in flood. After crossing the beck, keep right to reach the beach, then left along this back to Runswick Bay.

Points of interest

Runswick Bay – With its sweeping, sheltered bay and charming red roofed cottages, this is one of the Yorkshire coast's prettiest destinations. The sandy beach, which once provided anchorage for brightly coloured fishing boats, is now a family favourite for rock pooling, fossil hunting and coastal walks, where you can admire the breathtaking sea views.

9 Robin Hood's Bay

START At NZ950054, the station car park in Robin Hood's Bay, YO22 4RE

DISTANCE 6¾ miles (10.9 km)

SUMMARY Moderate walks mainly along disused railway lines and field paths

PARKING Pay and display car park

MAPS Explorer OL27; OS Sheets Landranger 94

WHERE TO EAT AND DRINK Various places in Robin Hood's Bay

A mixed walk along a disused railway line, woods and fields with fine views.

① From the car park, go right along Station Road, passing the old station to reach Thorpe Lane. Go right along this, where it turns left. Leave it by going up steps into a field. Go uphill through fields alongside Lingers Beck to emerge onto Church Lane beside houses. Go left along the lane, then right in front of Old Ridley onto Bedlington Lane, then left at the next junction onto Bowmans Lane to reach the village of Raw. Go right uphill along the road, then just after the telephone box, take the footpath on the left. Keep along a wet path alongside a wall to reach a road.

② Turn left, downhill and bear right at the junction and then through a gate leading to Fyling Hall School. Opposite, a wide track climbs steadily uphill through woods to eventually reach Ramsdale Mill Farm. Cross the bridge over Ramsdale Beck, and wall uphill alongside the edge of Carr Wood.

③ At the edge of this go left, pass through several fields (the path can be muddy in places) to reach Swallow Head Farm. Pass through the yard and follow the access track downhill to the road. Go right along this for a short distance to where the old railway line crosses it.

④ Go left onto the old track bed which is followed through trees, cross Middlehope Road and keep on to Thorpe Lane. Go right to re-join the outward route and retrace your footsteps back to the car park.

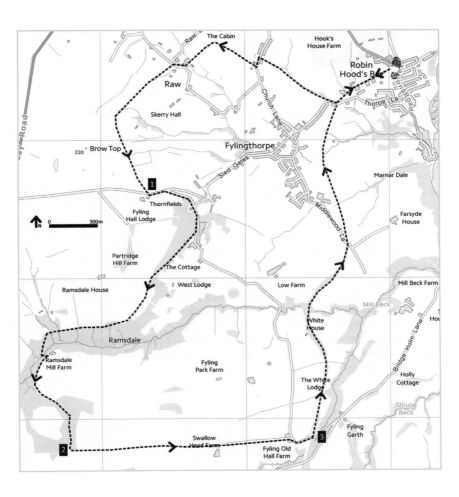

Points of interest

Robin Hood's Bay – A picturesque fishing village, which featured as Bramblewick in Leo Walmsley's book *Three Rivers*. The cliffs are well known to fossil hunters, but be warned – the tide rises fast!

10 Whitby

START At NZ898108, Whitby Tourist Information Centre, YO21 1YN

PARKING Pay and display car parking at the marina

DISTANCE 7 miles (11.25 km)

MAPS Explorer OL27; OS Sheets Landranger 94

SUMMARY A moderate walk mainly along disused railway lines and coastal paths

WHERE TO EAT AND DRINK Various places in Whitby

A fine walk starting in the historic town of Whitby, mainly along disused railway lines with grand views from the coastal paths.

1 From the TIC, go right along New Quay Road and then right over the Swing Bridge. Take the second left into Church Street. At the end, go right up the 199 steps to reach the abbey, pass through the car park and then go left onto the Cleveland Way path. Keep along the cliff top path, soon to reach the caravan park at Saltwick. Pass through this and keep left at the other side, staying on the Cleveland Way as far as the lighthouse.

2 Leave the Cleveland Way and go right along the road, then where it turns sharp right in front of a house, go left onto a bridleway across fields to Whitby Laithes Farm. Here, go right along the access track and then almost immediately, left through a gateway. Cross the field, then go right at the bottom to reach Hawkser Lane. Go left along this to a church, take the lane on the right behind the church which takes you to the A171. Cross this and keep straight ahead towards Stainsacre village.

3 Leave the road by taking the path on the left which gives access to the disused railway line. Go right along this underbridge and follow this towards Whitby. Keep on until you reach the viaduct over the River Esk. Cross this and, shortly after, the route is crossed by the Esk Valley Way.

4 Go right along the way, signposted to Whitby. Cross the school playing fields, then through the car park. Go right along the road towards the bridge – don't cross this. Cross the road and take the

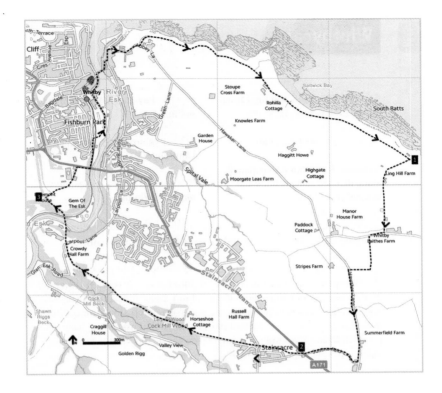

footpath leading down towards the marina. Go right after the first building and cross the railway tracks, then left along the banks of the River Esk back to the TIC.

Points of interest

Whitby – An extremely historic town, apart from its association with *Dracula*, whose trail can be followed. Many of the old shops sell jet, for which the town was a thriving centre. Captain Cook sailed from here. St Hilda founded the abbey in 657 AD. St Mary's Church was furnished largely by shipwrights and has likenesses to a sailing ship inside.

Start At NZ980016, National Trust Visitor Centre, YO13 0NE

Distance 7 miles (11.25 km)

Summary Moderate walks mainly along disused railway lines and moorland paths, which can be muddy in places

Parking Roadside parking on Raven Hill Road

Maps Explorer OL27; OS Sheets Landranger 94

Where to eat and drink National Trust Visitor Centre

A mixed walk along disused railway line and over open moorland with fine views.

[1] From the visitor centre, walk along Raven Hill Road, pass the church and then go right onto Robin Hood Road. Follow this to its end and then keep ahead, where it becomes unsurfaced to a marker post. Leave the track and take the path on the left uphill through gorse/heather alongside the fence. At the boundary stone, go left along a sunken lane to a road. Cross the road and take the right hand bridleway leading across Howldale Moor.

[2] After passing a small pond, the track forks. Keep right along the bridleway to reach The Ranch. Go through the farm yard and then downhill across fields to reach a track in a wooded area beside a stream.

[3] Go right along this track, passing buildings to Springhill Farm. Go left here, downhill along a fenced track. Follow this through woods to cross a footbridge at the bottom. The track then passes between fields to emerge into a farm yard. Pass straight through this onto a lane. Go right along the lane as far as a bridge over the disused railway line.

[4] Go left down a rough path just before the bridge to reach the track bed of the disused railway line. Then go right under the bridge and follow the track back towards Ravenscar, which is

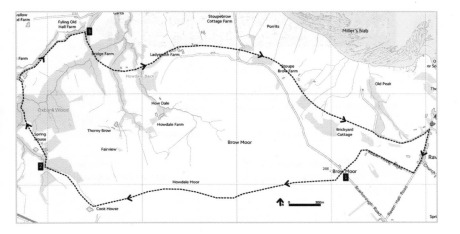

unfortunately all uphill. The first section is heavily wooded but after passing Brownside Farm, the trees disappear and there are good views along the coast towards both Robin Hood's Bay and Ravenscar. As you approach Ravenscar, the Cleveland Way footpath is crossed. At the signpost, keep right along a concrete track back to the visitor centre.

Points of interest

The National Trust Visitor Centre – This provides useful local information, including details of the Geological Trail around the old brick/mine workings in the area.

Robin Hood's Bay to Ravenscar

START At NZ950054, the station car park in Robin Hood's Bay, YO22 4RE

DISTANCE 8 miles (12.9 km)

SUMMARY Moderate walks mainly along disused railway lines and cliff top paths

PARKING Pay and display car park

MAPS Explorer OL27; OS Sheets Landranger 94

WHERE TO EAT AND DRINK Various places in Robin Hood's Bay

A varied walk along a disused railway returning along cliffs.

[1] From the car park, go along Station Road, passing the old station to reach Thorpe Lane. Go right along this to the old railway line. Go left onto this, the old track bed provides easy walking all the way to Ravenscar. Cross over Middlewood Lane, and then at the road crossing, go left to rejoin the old railway line. Just after this, a distinctive multi-arched bridge, which carries Bridge Holm Lane, is reached.

[2] Keep on the track back towards Ravenscar, which is unfortunately all uphill now. The first section after the bridge is heavily wooded but after passing Brownside Farm, the trees disappear and there are good views along the coast towards both Robin Hood's Bay and Ravenscar. As you approach Ravenscar, the Cleveland Way footpath is crossed.

[3] It's possible to go left onto the Cleveland Way here. To visit Ravenscar, keep on to reach a signpost. Here, go right along a concrete track to the visitor centre, which provides useful information about the local area and serves refreshments. Just past the centre, go left along the access road to the golf course. Keep on this as it loops downhill, with fine views back to Robin Hood's Bay, to re-join the Cleveland Way above a wooded ravine. Follow the cliff top path to reach a road opposite some cottages, go right along this to Stoupe Bank Farm. Keep straight on along the Cleveland Way to descend down into Boggle Hole.

[4] The path climbs steeply up from Boggle Hole via steps back up onto the tops of the cliffs. Keep on along the path heading back towards Robin

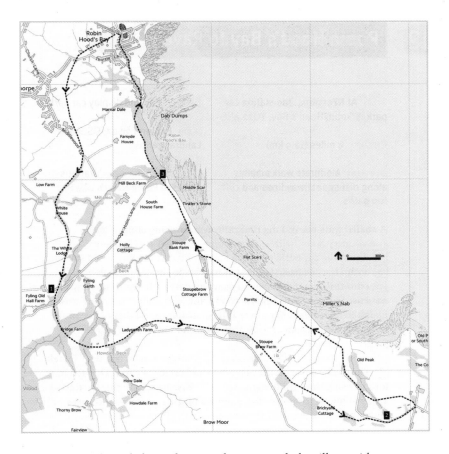

Hood's Bay. The path descends again when you reach the village, with steps bringing you out opposite The Bay Hotel. Go left along New Road, which is followed, uphill unfortunately, back to the car park.

Points of interest

Robin Hood's Bay – A picturesque fishing village, which featured as Bramblewick in Leo Walmsley's book *Three Rivers*. The cliffs are well known to fossil hunters, but be warned – the tide rises fast!

START At TA215695, Danes Dyke car park, YO15 1DU	PARKING Pay and display car park
DISTANCE 9 miles (14.5 km)	MAPS Explorer 301; OS Sheets Landranger 101
SUMMARY A difficult walk mainly along cliff top path and country lanes	WHERE TO EAT AND DRINK Various places in Flamborough village

A challenging walk along the cliffs, mainly along cliff top path and country lanes, with excellent opportunities for bird spotting.

1 From the car park, take the track on the east side which goes down to the shore. After a short distance, turn left along a narrower path. Follow this to the cliff top and walk east towards Flamborough Head. Take care and be aware of erosion, even though the cliffs appear to be safe. Descend the steps to reach South Landing.

2 Climb the steps on the other side and continue along the cliff tops to reach the lighthouse at Selwicks Bay. The chalk cliffs in the area provide nesting sites for many sea birds, and you will also see blow holes and caves below.

3 Keep along the cliff top path to reach North Landing.

4 The path goes past the car park and then down steps into a gully. Cross the fence at the top of the other side. Go left to houses, go behind these, and go along the side of another gully. Cross this and go right to reach Thornwick Bay. Descend and then climb steadily up North Cliff. Near the top, leave the cliff path by going left down through fields to reach the edge of Flamborough village.

5 At the track junction, go right and follow it past houses to reach a road. Go right along this and follow it into the village

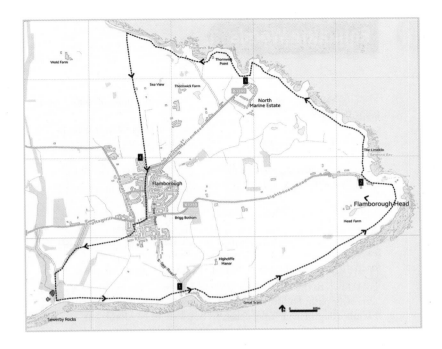

centre. At the T-junction, go right past the church, taking the first left into West Street, and then right into Water Lane. Where this turns sharp right, go left onto a footpath across fields to a road. Turn left along this and follow it back to the car park.

Points of interest

Flamborough Head – A chalk headland, with sheer white cliffs, Flamborough Head is eight miles long, between the Filey and Bridlington bays of the North Sea. The cliff top has two lighthouse towers; the oldest dates back to 1669 while Flamborough Head Lighthouse was built in 1806. In 1952, the older lighthouse was designated a Grade II listed building and is recorded in the National Heritage List for England. The cliffs are of international importance for their geology and among them, nesting sites for seabirds can be found.

14 Raincliffe Woods

START At SE984875, Green Gate car park, YO12 5TB

DISTANCE 9¼ miles (14.9 km)

SUMMARY A moderate walk mainly along field and woodland paths

PARKING Roadside car park

MAPS Explorer 27; OS Sheets Landranger 101

WHERE TO EAT AND DRINK None

A lovely walk through the Forge valley.

1 Leave the car park by taking the path on the SW corner which leads onto a forest road, follow this through the trees as far as a footpath on the right. Go right and shortly after descend down to a road. Go straight over this to a footbridge over the River Derwent. Cross and go right, follow the riverside path, keep on over several meadows to reach a road near to Cockran House.

2 Go right along the road, then right at the first junction, cross a bridge over the river then go right at the next junction, follow this road to Mowthorp Bridge.

3 Leave the road and go left through the farm yard to join Keld Runnels Road, a wide track leading uphill, to the edge of Holly Wood. Enter this and keep along the track, it descends slightly and soon widens as it passes a farm. The track eventually meets a road at Hay Brow. Go right along the road towards Scalby. To see the village, continue past the church ahead. Otherwise turn right at the junction to reach a bridge over the Sea Cut.

4 Cross this and take the path on the right running alongside the Sea Cut. Keep on this path until you are almost level with the point where Holly Wood comes down to the river, on the opposite bank.

5 Leave the riverside path here by going left across the field, on reaching a track in the fields, go L along it to a road. Go right

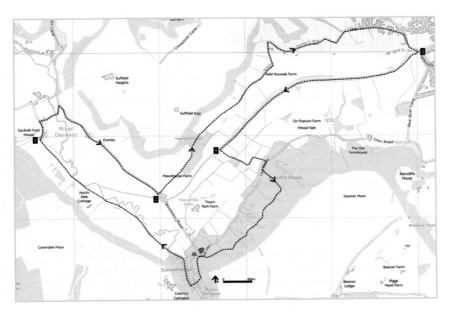

along the road, just before a dip in this, take the track leading uphill into Raincliffe Woods. Keep on uphill, ignoring any paths until a wide stony track (Middle Road) is reached. Turn right along this, follow it for about ¾ miles through the woods, where it forks, keep right downhill to reach the car park.

Points of interest

Forge Valley – The River Derwent cuts through this lovely valley on its long journey to the sea via the Humber. The 'Sea-Cut' helps prevent flooding by taking overflow from the Derwent to the sea via Scalby Beck. Look out for both herons and kingfishers along the banks of the river and sea cut.

15

16

Harland Moor

START At SE685909, Lowna, YO62 7JU

DISTANCE 2½ miles (4 km) or 4½ miles (7.2 km)

SUMMARY Easy walks, mainly along woodland and moorland tracks

PARKING Roadside parking

MAPS Explorer OL26; OS Sheets Landranger 94

WHERE TO EAT AND DRINK None

Two lovely walks through woods and over heather moorlands.

1 From the parking, walk north along the track into woodland to a footbridge. Cross this and keep on between walls to the Quaker burial grounds, on your left, at a lovely peaceful spot. On over open ground now to where the wall on your right turns sharp right, follow downhill to the banks of the River Dove. Don't cross it, turn left and follow it upstream to Dale End Bridge. Leave the riverbank and climb up the path on the left to reach a track.

2 Go left along this and follow it to a road, then left along the road until a footpath sign on the right is reached. Leave the road and go downhill over two fields to Harland Beck Farm. Go through the gate directly ahead, then diagonally right across the field to enter woodland. Cross a stream and follow the path through the woods to a track junction. Go left a short distance to a second junction.

3 Go left along the track between fields. Pass the farm at Faddell Rigg to reach the road. Go left along it back to the parking area.

4 For the longer walk, cross the track and go diagonally right along a narrow path uphill over heather moors to reach a road. Cross over onto a wide track. Follow this over moorland, it curves to the right towards trees. Cross a stream, then left along a wall to a gate. Go left through this and follow the path over rough pasture to a road.

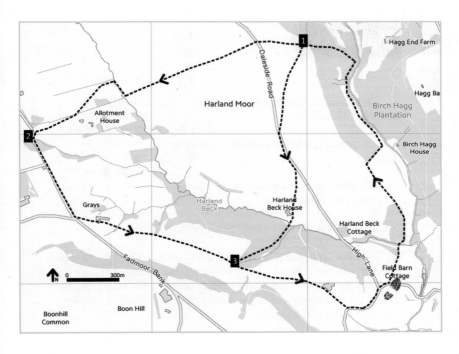

⑤ Go left along the road and follow it to a T-junction. Leave the road here and go left over a field to Grays Farm. Pass between the buildings and go diagonally right towards a gate. Pass through this into the field. Keep ahead to the corner of a fence. Keep ahead with the fence on your right and follow the track over fields to the corner of the woods.

Points of interest

Stone circle – On Harland Moor there is a stone circle consisting of twelve edge-set boulders. It has a hollow in the centre thought to be a medieval ore-pit. To the south lies a cairn field and a stone that I believe to be an outlier to the circle.

May Beck

START At NZ892024, May Beck car park, YO22 5JE

DISTANCE 3 miles (4.8 km) or 6 miles (9.6 km)

SUMMARY Moderate walks mainly along woodland paths/tracks

PARKING Forest car park

MAPS Explorer OL27; OS Sheets Landranger 94

WHERE TO EAT AND DRINK None

Two fine walks around the wooded May Beck valley.

1️⃣ From the car park, cross over May Beck and take the signed footpath along the east bank. Follow the path through the woods for about 1 mile until Foss Lane is met. Cross straight over this and keep along the eastern side of May Beck. Keep on until a track comes in from the left near to the edge of the woods.

2️⃣ Go left and follow the track downhill through the woods. Cross the river in the valley bottom and keep right, heading uphill through the woods to reach Leas Head Farm. Leave the woods, go through a field and pass to the right of the farm buildings. Walk past the front of the farm, cross its access track and then go to the left of the buildings into the woods for a short distance. Keep ahead across the field to join a track, go left along this to Foss Farm. Pass to the left of the buildings to enter woods once again. Go left along a track for a short distance, leaving it by going right onto another track. Keep on through the woods, where the path forks. Keep right to follow the edge of the woods into a clearing.

3️⃣ Go left along a path into the trees which is followed down to the car park.

4️⃣ For the longer walk, keep straight ahead through the clearing. Where the fence turns right, keep directly ahead to join a track. Go left along this until a smaller track goes off on the right. Go right here and follow the track through the trees to a T-junction.

⑤ Go left and then take a fainter path going off on the left before the track turns. Keep along this path, cross a track and keep on in the same direction through woods to a ruined building, John Bonds Sheep House. Shortly after this, exit the woods and go left along the edge of them. The path bends away from the trees to join a track. Go left along this to a T-junction, go left here and follow it downhill. Where the track starts to bear away from the trees, leave it and keep left. Pass through a field, and then downhill to the road. Go left back over May Beck to the car park.

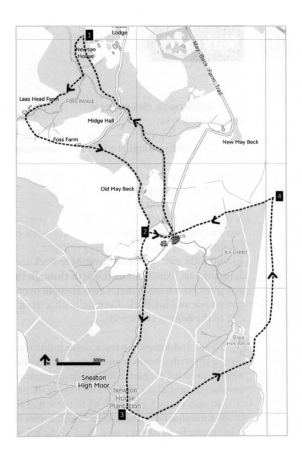

Points of interest

Falling Foss – At 67 feet high, it is one of Yorkshire's highest waterfalls. It is located in a lovely wooded valley about 5 miles south of Whitby.

START At SE744858, St Gregory's Minster, YO62 7TZ

DISTANCE 3¾ miles (6 km)

SUMMARY An easy walk mainly along field and woodland paths

PARKING Limited roadside parking

MAPS Explorer OL26; OS Sheets Landranger 100

WHERE TO EAT AND DRINK None

A fine walk through Kirkdale, the lower part of Bransdale.

1️⃣ From the church, walk along the lane, going through the gate at the end into the field. Cross this to Hodge Beck, cross the ford and continue across the field beyond to the edge of woods. Enter these on a track, going left, as the track starts to veer right into Kirkdale Howl. Leave it and go left into a field. Go along the edge of woods, to enter them at the end of the field.

2️⃣ Keep on through the woods, alongside Hodge Beck – the path climbs to reach a track junction. Go left and keep climbing through the woods. Bear left at the next junction of track to reach the edge of the woods.

3️⃣ Go diagonally left across the field to a track. Go right along this and then left at the end of the field. Follow the track over fields, going right at the next junction to reach Starfits Lane, beside Low Hagg Farm. Go left along the road, then right at the junction. Keep along the road and pass Hagg Farm to enter woods.

4️⃣ Keep on along the road through the woods to a track leading off on the right. Leave the road here and go right onto the track through Robin Hood's Howl. Where the track doubles back on itself, leave it and keep on heading south through the woods. At the end of the woods, go diagonally right across the field, pass the end of a hedge/fence and keep on in the same direction to reach Starfits Lane again. Go left to the crossroads, then go right and follow the road, past Kirkdake Cave to junction. Go right back to the church.

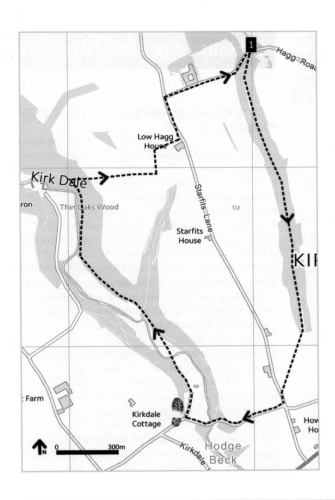

Points of interest

St Gregory's Minster, in Kirkdale near Kirkbymoorside, is an Anglo-Saxon church with a rare sundial. The church was built around 1060 on the site of an earlier church, and is dedicated to St Gregory, pope from 590 to 604.

Captain Cook's and Highcliff Nab

START At NZ592110, Gribdale Gate, YO21 2RU

DISTANCE 3¾ miles (6 km) or 8½ miles (13.7 km)

SUMMARY Moderate walks along moorland and forest paths

PARKING Roadside car park

MAPS OS Sheets Landranger 93

WHERE TO EAT AND DRINK None

Two beautiful walks around Great Ayton Moors with grand viewpoints.

1 From the car park, go south along the Cleveland Way, climbing along a wide track through trees. Keep ahead to reach Captain Cook's Monument. Go left in front of this and follow the path over heather moors to a gap in the wall. Go down a stone pitched path to join a track, go left along this and follow it, keeping right where the Cleveland Way leaves it. Keep on through the woods to reach a road. Go left on this and follow it downhill into Lonsdale. Where it turns left, keep ahead and climb a track alongside trees to reach a gate on the edge of the moors.

2 Go through the gate and then take the track on the left and follow this around the head of Lonsdale back to the car park.

3 For the longer walk, at the head of Lonsdale, go right along the road and follow it over Percy Cross Rigg to a track going off on the left. Go along this to Sleddale Farm. Go left here before the gate and follow the track over Codhill Heights to a gate on the edge of woods.

4 Go through the gate and follow the path to join a forest track. Go left along this, passing the outcrop of Highcliff Nab, on your right. At the next junction, go left and follow the forest track through the woods, it contours the wooded slopes. Keep on until after the fourth track going off on your right. Just after this, there is a path leading uphill on the left. Go up this to the large boulder, the Hanging Stone, pass it and keep on another forest track. Go right along this, exit the woods to a gate on the corner of Newton Moor, for the fine views of Roseberry Topping.

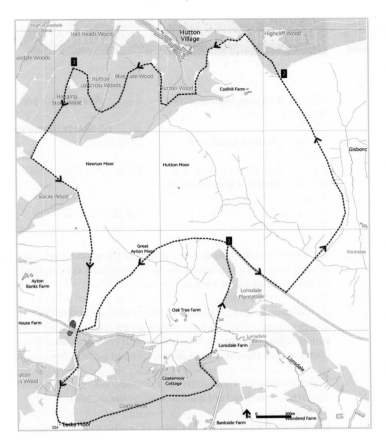

⑤ Go left along the Cleveland Way, following the fence line over the moors back to the parking area.

Points of interest

Captain Cook's Monument – A well-known local landmark which stands on Easby Moor, at over 1,300 feet, can be seen for miles around. It's dedicated to the memory of the celebrated explorer, James Cook, who was born and lived in the area.

The Bridestones

START At SE883903, High Staindale car park, YO18 7LR

DISTANCE 4 miles (6.5 km)

SUMMARY A moderate walk mainly along moorland and woodland paths

PARKING Forestry car park

MAPS Explorer OL27; OS Sheets Landranger 100

WHERE TO EAT AND DRINK None

A short walk linked to make a grand walk through the Dalby Forest.

① Exit the car park from its western end along a footpath. Keep along this, passing Staindale Lake to join the road. Go left along it, pass the toilets to a car park on the right.

② Go through the car park, and follow the path leading uphill into the woods to the edge of an open area beside a stream. Take the path leading diagonally left up through the trees and out onto the open ground. The path turns sharp right and heads north over the open ground soon to reach the sandstone outcrops. Keep straight ahead, heading north, over Low Bridestones, keeping left where the path curves around the head of Bridestones Griff. Go left at the junctions and follow the path downhill into Dove Dale. At the bottom, keep left along the bottom edge of the woods, to re-join your outward route. Go right back to the car park.

③ Cross the road into the car park opposite, exiting over the footbridge at the rear of this. Follow the path up through the trees to a road. Go right along the road, to just before the hair pin bend. Here, go left along a track and follow it over Adderstone Rigg. Keep on along the track, ignoring any paths/tracks on the right to round the head of Worry Gill. Keep on to the sharp right turn in the track. Soon afterwards, take the path on the left leading down through the trees to another track. Go right along it and cross the stream to pass a house back to the car park.

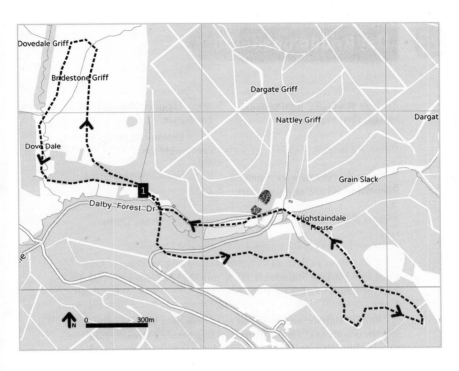

Points of interest

The Bridestones – Or 'Brink-stones' or edge stones in Old Norse. These fascinating rocks are the remains of a sandstone 'cap' that was originally much higher, Jurassic sedimentary rock deposited some 150 million years ago. Layers of hard sandstone alternating with softer calcareous layers have been eroded by wind, frost and rain over thousands of years. The result is the strange and wonderful shapes left today.

23 Danby and Castleton

START At NZ684083, Castleton village, YO21 2EU

MAPS Explorer OL26; OS Sheets Landranger 94

DISTANCE 4½ miles (7.25 km)

SUMMARY An easy walk mainly along field and woodland paths

WHERE TO EAT AND DRINK The Eskdale Inn
http://www.theeskdalecastleton.co.uk

PARKING Roadside parking

A fine walk linking the villages of Danby and Castleton.

1 From the parking area, go right along the road past the play area. Continue uphill along the footpath. Where the road curves left, go ahead on a path between the buildings to emerge at a T-junction. Go down steps, cross the road and go left along Church Street. Keep on past the church, and then go right onto a footpath at the end of the houses. Follow this down to cross a footbridge and climb up the other bank to the war memorial. At the road, go right on a rough track to the entrance of Howe Farm.

2 Go through the gate and directly across the yard to exit via a gate opposite. Go right along the wall, cross a ladder stile, then left along the field edge to reach a road, opposite Danby Vicarage. Go left along the road, then right along a footpath, passing between barns to cross a stile into a field. Go left along the stream across fields to a stile in front of houses. Cross this and then go right along the road into Ainthorpe village. Keep left where the road forks to reach a T-junction opposite the fire station.

3 Go right along the road and follow it into Danby village, then go left opposite the Duke of Wellington pub. Keep on to a footpath sign on the right, leave the road here and go right along the wall to join a track. Go right towards Hollin Top Farm, and pass to the right of the buildings, along a walled lane to a gate leading onto open moorlands.

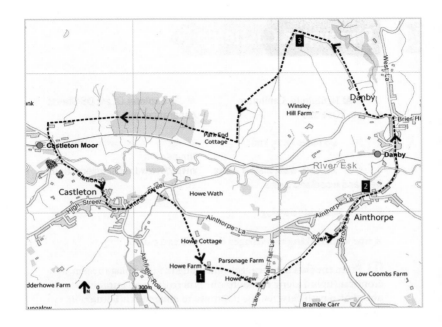

4 Go through this and walk a short distance, then go left through a gate into another walled lane. Keep along this to another gate, exit the lane and shortly after the path forks, keep right over open moorland. The path descends to a gate, go through this and follow the wall downhill to the corner of a wall. Go diagonally right across open grass to join a track on the edge of Danby Park. Go right along the track into the woods, follow the path through the woods to exit via a gate. Keep along the track to buildings on your left. At the end of these, descend stone steps to reach the road. Go left under the railway bridge and follow the road back to the parking area.

Points of interest

Danby Castle – A fourteenth century castle, once the home of Katherine Parr (the last wife of Henry VIII) is now a farm, located one mile east of Danby village.

START At SE744858, Sinnington
village, YO62 6RY

DISTANCE 4½ miles (7.25 km)

SUMMARY An easy walk mainly along
field and woodland paths

PARKING Roadside parking

MAPS Explorer OL26; OS Sheets
Landranger 100

WHERE TO EAT AND DRINK The Fox and
Hounds Inn
www.thefoxandhoundsinn.co.uk

A fine walk linking two villages by woodland paths.

[1] From the parking area at the north end of the village green,
cross the River Severn via the bridge and go right in front of the
houses. Keep on this track as it follows the river, first through
woods and then fields to reach a wooden gate. Leave the track and
go right into the woods. After passing through a newly planted
area of woodland, go through a gate into a field and go left uphill
alongside the hedge to reach Appleton-le-Moors village.

[2] Go right along the road through the village. Soon after
passing the church, a road junction is reached. Go right here onto
Hamley Lane and follow this downhill to where it turns sharp
left. Leave the road and take the track downhill, heading towards
Appleton Mill Farm. At the bottom of the hill, keep right to enter
the farm yard. Go right into a field in front of the farmhouse and
keep left along the field edge to reach the ford across the River
Severn.

[3] Under normal river levels, it's easy enough to cross the stream,
but could be difficult in flood conditions so caution is advised. On
the opposite bank, pass the white washed farmhouse, then go left
uphill to a gate, pass through this and then go right onto a path
through the woods. In the spring, these woods are carpeted with
wild garlic and bluebells. Keep on through the woods. At a fork
in the path, go right to reach a gate on the edge of the woods. Exit

into the field, going downhill and through another gate on the right into a riverside pasture. Go left across the pasture to a gate. Go through this onto a track leading up into woods. Keep straight ahead at the cross path to reach a lane beside a house. Go right along this back into Sinnington Village.

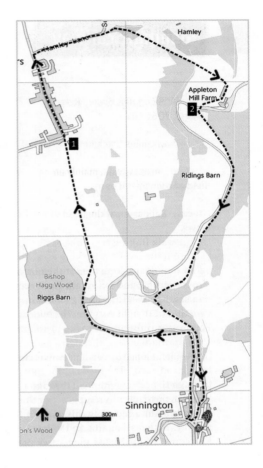

Rosedale Railway

START At SE683989, Blakey Ridge, YO62 7LQ

DISTANCE 4¾ miles (7.6 km)

SUMMARY An easy walk, mainly on disused railway tracks

PARKING Roadside parking

MAPS Explorer 26; OS Sheets Landranger 94

WHERE TO EAT AND DRINK The Lion Inn http://www.lionblakey.co.uk

An easy walk around the head of the Rosedale valley with fine views.

(1) From the roadside parking area, head east towards the Rosedale valley over grass, soon to reach the track bed of the old railway. Cross over this and follow the path steeply down, through bracken and heather towards Moorlands Farm. Go through a gate into the yard and bear right between the buildings to join its access road. Follow this through the valley to a T-junction.

(2) Go left along the road, pass Red House Farm, and keep on to Dale Head Farm. The road climbs into the farm yard. After going through the gate, go immediately right to pass to the right of a large barn. The path climbs steeply along the edge of woodlands. When these thin out, keep on uphill to reach the track bed of the disused railway. Go left along this and follow it as it curves around Nab Scar. Keep on until the large embankment across Reeking Gill is reached.

(3) From here, the going underfoot gets wetter as the old track bed has become waterlogged in places. Climb up the left side of the cutting and follow the path to avoid a boggy section, descending back to the track bed again. Keep following it, avoiding the worst of the boggy bits. As the head of the valley is in reach, the track bed climbs slightly and then it becomes drier underfoot. The views down the valley are stunning on a clear day. Keep on following the old railway, passing disused buildings to reach the point where you descend from the car park at the start of the walk. Go right back uphill over grass to the parking area.

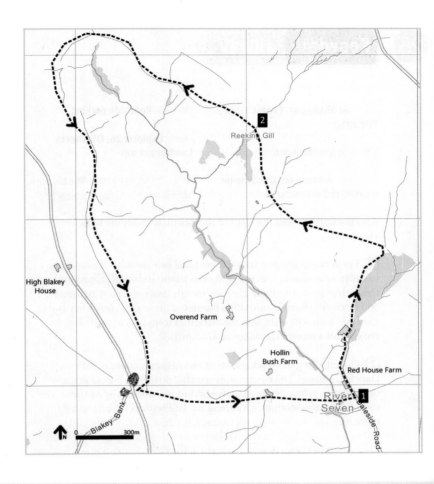

Points of interest

🔍 Rosedale Railway – The eleven mile, goods-only railway line
opened in 1861 to transport the iron ore mined in the valley over to
the steel works at Teesside. It ran across the heights of the North
York Moors, from Battersby Junction to the Rosedale valley. The line closed
in 1929.

26 **Kepwick**

START At SE466907, Kepwick village, YO7 2JP

DISTANCE 5 miles (8 km)

SUMMARY A moderate walk, mainly on field and moorland paths

PARKING Roadside parking

MAPS Explorer 26; OS Sheets Landranger 100

WHERE TO EAT AND DRINK None

A walk along the western edge of the North York Moors with fine views.

1 Go through the gate into the field and head south, climbing towards Atley Bank. Exit the field onto moorlands. Still climbing, the path bears to the right, then follows the wall uphill, with forest on either side. Keep on climbing alongside the wall. It turns left and then right. Shortly after this, a junction of tracks is reached close to the edge of a forest plantation on Gallow Hill.

2 Go left along the track, heading away from the forest, then climbing across Clarke Scars to reach the wall at the top. Cross this onto a track running alongside it. Go left along this. At the crossroads keep straight ahead, until a wall leading off on the left is reached.

3 Go left here and descend alongside the wall. At the bottom, keep to the right of trees to shortly afterwards enter a field. Follow the track over the stream. It then turns left to pass Nab Farm. Keep on the track to reach Bridge Beck Lane.

4 Go left along the lane back towards Kepwick. On entering the village, keep right at the junction and follow the road past the houses back to the start.

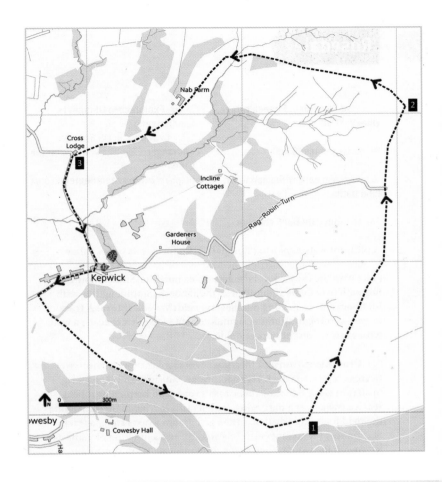

Points of interest

The Hambleton Hills – A range of hills, formed on the western edge of the North York Moors, separated by the valley of the River Rye. They are east of the Vale of Mowbray, which borders an escarpment. They run in a north-south direction for fifteen miles and merge with the Cleveland Hills (north) and Howardian Hills (south).

27 Rosedale

START At SE723959, Rosedale village, YO18 8RA

DISTANCE 5 miles (8 km)

SUMMARY An easy walk, mainly on field paths

PARKING Heygate Bank car park

MAPS Explorer 26; OS Sheets Landranger 94

WHERE TO EAT AND DRINK Graze on the Green http://www.grazeonthegreen.co.uk

A pleasant walk exploring Rosedale, with fine views of the valley.

1 Leave the car park via the gate on its north side and follow the footpath over fields alongside Northdale Beck. Stay along this path for about a mile, passing over several fields via gates/stiles. A track is joined, coming in from the right. Keep left along this to reach a wall with a stream on the opposite side.

2 Cross the stream and then go diagonally left downhill into woods to cross Northdale Beck via a footbridge. Go right and then go right upstream alongside the beck. Cross a road, and keep on over fields to reach a track near a barn. Go left along this to a road. Go right along the road for a short distance, then go left into woods along a track. Stay on this for about ½ mile to a stream, and a junction of paths. Go left to exit the woods, then pass Clough House. Keep along its access track to a junction. Here, go left downhill to a road.

3 Go right along the road, then left into Craven Garth Farm. Pass through its yard onto a path over fields. Keep on downhill to cross a stream, then shortly after this join a walled track. Go left along it and follow it to the road at Thorgill.

4 Go left along the road for about ½ mile, then go left over a field to cross a stream via a footbridge. Go right and follow the path over fields to enter a caravan park. Keep left to join the road and follow this back into the centre of the village.

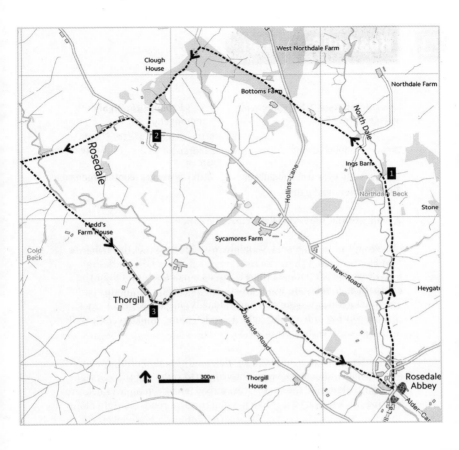

Points of interest

Rosedale Abbey – Founded in 1158, the original priory was inhabited by nuns who were the first to farm sheep commercially in the region. In 1535, the priory ceased its operations as a result of the Dissolution of the Monasteries. By the nineteenth century, the building was dismantled when the stone was reclaimed for building, including a new church on the original priory's site. A staircase, a sundial and a single stone pillar are all that remains.

28 Head of Farndale

START At Gill Beck, NZ643002, YO62 7LH

DISTANCE 5 miles (8 km)

SUMMARY An easy walk, mainly on field and moorland paths

PARKING Roadside parking

MAPS Explorer 26; OS Sheets Landranger 94

WHERE TO EAT AND DRINK None

A walk around the head of the Farndale valley.

(1) From the parking area, walk north-west along the road towards Elm House Farm. Where the road turns left to the farm buildings, leave it and go right onto a track between stone walls into a field. Cross the field then exit onto open moors, the track climbing alongside the tree lined Gill Beck, on your right. Where the track turns to the left, leave it and keep directly ahead, climbing over moors to reach the track bed of the old Rosedale Ironstone Railway.

(2) Go left along this and follow it as it contours around the head of the valley towards Bloworth Crossing. The views back down the Farndale valley are outstanding, on a clear day. Keep onto a track junction on Rudland Rigg.

(3) Go left at the crossroads, heading south-east along Rudland Rigg. Ignore the track going off on the right, keep on to a line of grouse butts descending the moors on your left. Leave the track and follow the line of butts downhill. At the end of these, aim diagonally right over the moors towards the walls in the valley bottom to reach a gate. Go through this into rough pasture, cross the infant River Dove, then pass between stone walls to follow a tumbledown stone wall eastwards. Keep on the end of the wall near to a large tree and a barn.

(4) Go diagonally right to cross a stream in the trees, to then join Daleside Road. Keep along this to reach Elm House Farm again. Go past the farm and follow the road back to the parking area.

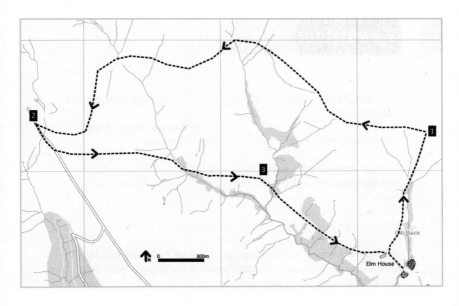

Points of interest

Rosedale Railway – The 11 mile, goods-only railway line opened in 1861 to transport the iron ore mined in the valley over to the steel works at Teesside. It ran across the heights of the North York Moors, from Battersby Junction to the Rosedale valley. The line closed in 1929.

29 Howldale

START At SE834830, Thornton-le-Dale, YO18 7LF

DISTANCE 5½ miles (9 km)

SUMMARY An easy walk, mainly on field and woodland paths, which can be muddy

PARKING Pay and display car park

MAPS Explorer 27; OS Sheets Landranger 100

WHERE TO EAT AND DRINK Various places in Thornton-le-Dale

A pleasant walk exploring around Thornton-le-Dale.

1 From the centre of the village, go left along Pickering Road at the A170 and follow this until the junction with Greengates Lane. Just after this, go right into a field, going diagonally left over this. Keep on in the same direction to join a track, beside a tree. Go right along the track for a short distance, then across a field towards woods. Go through these to cross a track in front of Haggs House. Keep ahead to a junction of paths at the head of Howl Dale.

2 Go right and follow the path through the wooded Howl Dale valley. Keep on to a T-junction of paths.

3 Go right into Orchan Dale, and then right again at the next junction to exit the woods. Keep along this track, over fields to reach a road. Go left along the road to a T-junction, go right here and follow it to where a track goes off to the right into woods. Leave the road here and take the right. Follow this, then over open ground to reach the Ellerburn Road beside a church.

4 Go right along the road to a junction with Priestman's Lane, keep right again here. At the junction with Whitby Gate, go left and follow the road back into the centre of the village.

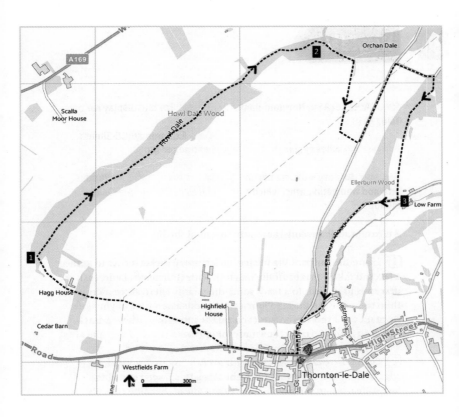

Points of interest

Thornton-le-Dale – Often regarded as one of the prettiest in Yorkshire. One of its cottages has appeared on countless calendars and chocolate boxes over the years. The village is also famous for its annual show where people from the area gather to compete in various events.

30 Bilsdale

START At SE564889, Newgate Bank, YO62 5LT

DISTANCE 5¾ miles (9.2 km)

SUMMARY An easy walk, mainly on woodland paths, which can be muddy

PARKING Forestry car park

MAPS Explorer 26; OS Sheets Landranger 93

WHERE TO EAT AND DRINK None

An easy walk exploring the southern end of the Bilsdale valley.

(1) Leave the car park via the path in the north-west corner to join a forest track. Go right along this, following it through the trees. It descends to the left, to a track junction, go right here. Keep along this track, now with open views over the Bilsdale valley to your left. Keep on until you reach the corner of the moorland, where a track comes in from the right, down Rievaulx Bank.

(2) Go left here and follow the path over the moors, along the edge of the trees to a track. Go right along this, keep right at the fork to reach a crossroads. Keep straight ahead, heading roughly southwards, through the trees. After exiting the trees, a parking area, on your left, is reached.

(3) Leave the road and go right along a good track. Follow this along the edge of Rievaulx moor and the trees back to the entrance road to the car park.

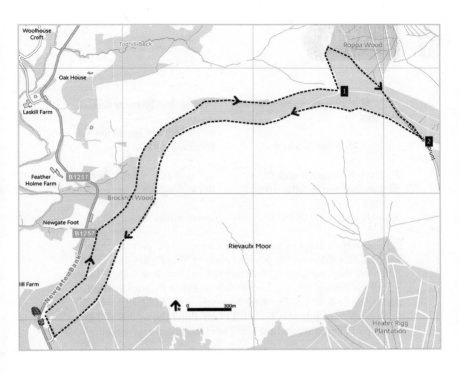

Points of interest

Bilsdale – The place name is derived from Old Norse, Bildr, which means 'Bildr's valley.' Hasty Bank is at the head of the dale, and this extends ten miles south to meet Rye Dale. The dale is the valley of the River Seph, which forms where Raisdale Beck joins Bilsdale Beck at Chop Gate in the north of the dale. The River Seph flows south, meeting the River Rye at Seph Mouth.

START At NZ477020, Swainby village, DL6 3DG

DISTANCE 5¾ miles (9.2 km)

SUMMARY A moderate walk mainly on moorland and woodland paths

PARKING Roadside car park

MAPS Explorer 26; OS Sheets Landranger 93

WHERE TO EAT AND DRINK The Black Horse, Swainby

A lovely walk around the Scugdale valley with fine views.

[1] Leave the village by going along Church Lane, past the church. Keep on along the road to pass the ruins of Whorlton Castle. Keep following the road until it turns just before Whorlton village. Leave it here, go through the gate on the left, and then diagonally right across the field, to a hedge. Keep along the right hand edge of fields to a corner of woods at Whorl Hill Farm. Enter the woods and keep to the path, going around the left side of the hill to emerge onto Bank Lane.

[2] Go right along the track and follow it to enter another wood, climb up through these. At the top, exit the woods and go left along the wall along a path. Follow this as gently climbs up to the right to join the Cleveland Way on Live Moor.

[3] Go right along the Cleveland Way, over open moorland, then descend steeply over Knolls End. At the bottom of the descent, keep left along the edge of the woods to reach the road at Huthwaite Green. Go straight over the crossroads to pass Hollin Hill Farm and keep on to where the road crosses Scugdale Beck.

[4] Cross the beck and then leave the road. Go right uphill across a field to enter woodland again, bear right in the woods and follow the track. Where this bears sharp left, keep straight ahead to shortly leave the woods to join a road. Go right along the road and follow it back into Swainby village.

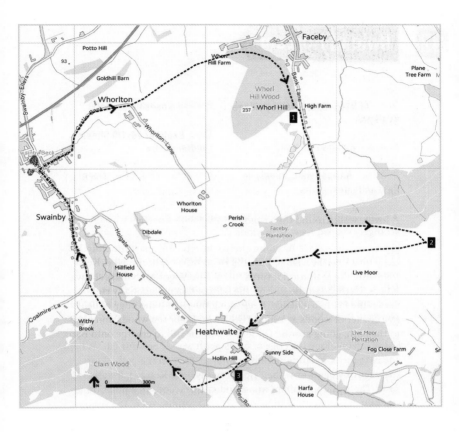

Points of interest

🔍 Whorlton Castle – A ruined medieval castle situated near Whorlton, built in the twelfth century as a Norman motte-and-bailey associated with the nearby settlement. All that remains of the castle are some cellars or undercrofts. A fourteenth century gatehouse still survives, albeit in poor condition.

START At SE852937, Hole of Horcum, YO18 7NR

PARKING Layby on the A169

MAPS Explorer 27; OS Sheets Landranger 94

DISTANCE 6 miles (9.6 km)

SUMMARY An easy walk, mainly on field and forest paths

WHERE TO EAT AND DRINK None

An interesting walk to the Bridestones Nature Reverse, with its strangely shaped rock formations.

1 From the layby, go right along the A169, a short distance to the track Old Wife's Way, going off on the right. Go along this and follow it to where it turns towards Newgate Foot Farm. Leave it here and keep straight ahead along a path, running along the top of Newgate Brow. Keep ahead to where a footpath comes in on the left.

2 Keep on along the edge of fields, with woods on your left. Where the path forks, keep right onto moorland. Stay on the path along the edge of what is now the Bridestones Nature Reserve, for about 1 mile. The path then enters woodland and descends to a junction of tracks.

3 Take the path leading diagonally right up through the trees and out onto the open ground. The path turns sharp right and heads north over the open ground, soon to reach the sandstone outcrops. Keep straight ahead, heading north, over Low Bridestones, keeping left where the path curves around the head of Bridestones Griff. At the track junction, go right along High Bridestones, heading north. The path follows the east side of Dovedale Gill. Where the gill bears to the left, keep along it to reach a pond in the corner of a field. Go diagonally right across the field to join the track from the outward route on Newgate Brow.

4 Go left and re-trace your outward route back to the layby.

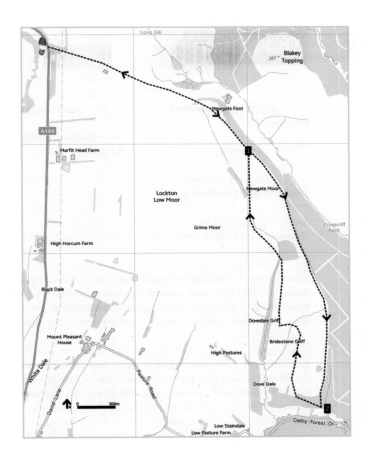

Points of interest

The Bridestones – Or 'Brink-stones' or edge stones in Old Norse. These fascinating rocks are the remains of a sandstone 'cap' that was originally much higher, Jurassic sedimentary rock deposited some 150 million years ago. Layers of hard sandstone alternating with softer calcareous layers have been eroded by wind, frost and rain over thousands of years. The result is the strange and wonderful shapes left today.

33 Osmotherly

START At SE469994, Cod Beck
Reservoir, DL6 3AL

DISTANCE 6 miles (9.7 km)

SUMMARY A moderate walk mainly
moorland paths with sections on
roads

PARKING Roadside car park

MAPS Explorer 26; OS Sheets
Landranger 99

WHERE TO EAT AND DRINK None

A scenic walk around the Cod Beck valley to the north of
Osmotherly.

[1] Exit the car park and go right along the road to a track on the
right. Go right here, over a footbridge and climb along a rocky eroded
track. Keep along this track alongside a plantation, at the end of the
trees keep ahead, with good views of Black Hambleton, to where the
wall ends.

[2] Leave the road and go right along a track running beside a
fence/wall. Where this turns left, follow it downhill to the road. Go
right along this and follow it to a cattle grid, cross and then go right
through a gate into a field. Follow the right edge of the field down to
a track, where the Cleveland Way is joined. Go through a stile and
continue along a track towards Whitehouse Farm. Go right before the
buildings and follow a path downhill over fields to cross Slapestones
Beck, via a footbridge in the valley bottom. Climb steps up through
woods. At the top, exit the woods and follow a stone pitched path
across fields into Osmotherly. On reaching the road, cross it and
follow a narrow path directly ahead through houses to emerge onto
the main street.

[3] Go right along Quarry Lane, follow this uphill through the
village. At the top of the climb, go left onto Rueberry Lane, passing
houses. Keep left where the track forks to reach Chapel Wood Farm.
Go through a kissing gate on the right and cross three fields to a gate
on the edge of woodlands.

④ Go through the gate and take the right fork uphill through mixed Birch/Oak trees, with fine views left over the Vale of York. Pass radio masts and keep ahead to a gate on the edge of the woods. Exit the woods and follow a stone pitched path over open moorland to reach a road. Go right along this and follow it back to the car park.

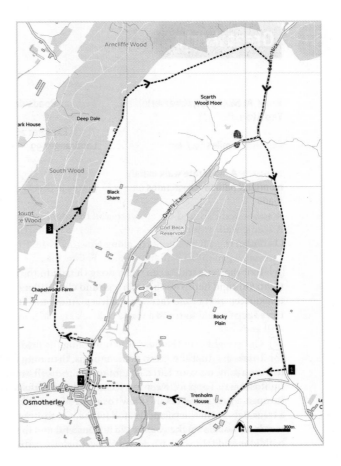

Points of interest

Cod Beck Reservoir – This is a man-made lake situated within the North York Moors National Park and near the village of Osmotherley. The reservoir is named after Cod Beck, which is the small river that fills it. It was built to supply drinking water to the local area via a treatment works, but these have now closed due to poor water quality.

Great Ayton

START At NZ563107, Great Ayton TIC, TS9 6BJ

DISTANCE 6 miles (9.6 km)

SUMMARY A moderate walk mainly on moorland and forest paths

PARKING Roadside parking

MAPS Explorer 26; OS Sheets Landranger 93

WHERE TO EAT AND DRINK Various places in Great Ayton village

A scenic walk around Great Ayton and the moors above.

1 From the TIC, walk north along Newton Road, then go right through a gap in the wall into woods. Follow the path through the grounds of Cleveland Lodge, then across a field to the railway line. Cross this and climb up through a field to Cliff Ridge Woods. Go diagonally right uphill through the trees. At the top keep left along the edge of a field to reach a track.

2 Go straight over the track junction along the field edge, aiming for Roseberry Topping. Keep on over fields, then onto open ground to pass a folly, on your left. Go right to join the well-trodden path up Roseberry Topping. Keep left where the path forks to reach the summit. There are extensive views over Teesside from the top, on a clear day. From the trig point, follow the stone pitched path that winds its way down the eastern ridge. Descend and then follow the path alongside the wall. Climb up to a gate on the corner of Newton Moor.

3 Go right along the edge of the woods and follow the Cleveland Way path to the car park at Gribdale Gate. Go through the gate and climb up through the trees, still on the Cleveland Way to reach Captain Cook's Monument.

4 There are many paths radiating away from the monument, in every direction. Head north-west to reach the corner of a wall, follow the path alongside this to a corner. Go left and follow a path down into woodland, keeping right where the path forks. Cross a track in

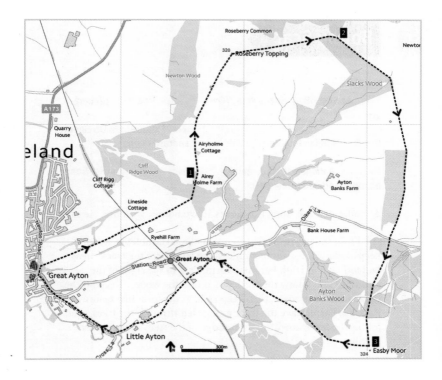

the woods, keep on a short distance to reach a wall. Go left along this, and at the corner go right onto another track. Keep along this, to pass a house on your left. Just after this, go left onto a track. Follow this, over the railway line to Brookside Farm. Pass to the right of the buildings and keep on to the junction with Cross Lane. Go right along the road and follow it back into Great Ayton.

Points of interest

Airy Holme Farm – James Cook came to live at the farm, when he was eight years old, his father being the local bailiff.

35 Boltby Scar

Start At SE509876, Sneck Yate, YO7 2HP

Distance 6 miles (9.6 km)

Summary A moderate walk mainly on moorland and forest paths

Parking Roadside parking

Maps Explorer 26; OS Sheets Landranger 99

Where to eat and drink None

A moderate walk along the moors above Boltby, with fine views.

1 From the parking area, go north along Hambleton Road, keep along this for about a mile. Keep left where the track turns and follow it to High Paradise Farm. Pass to the right of the buildings and follow the track down into the woods. Keep on the track, it passes houses, then keep right at the fork. Just before Low Paradise Farm, leave the track and go left through the trees, then follow the fence downhill to the edge of the trees in the valley bottom.

2 Go diagonally left across the field, cross a track in the woods, keep on over rough pastures for roughly ¼ mile to join a track. Go left along this and follow to a road. Keep right onto the road and follow it into Boltby village.

3 Take the first road on the left, follow this over fields to the edge of Cow Pasture Wood. Enter these and keep along the track to a wall. Go left uphill and follow the edge of the trees over Little Moor. Cross a track, keep ahead through a gap in the trees. The path turns to the right, keep on to reach the edge of the trees. Shortly beyond this is a track junction.

4 Go left along this track and follow over Boltby Scar, there are fine views down into the Vale of York to the left. You will pass many of the earthworks of the ancient iron ages sites. Pass High Barn and keep along the edge of fields to reach the road. Go right and follow this uphill back to the parking area.

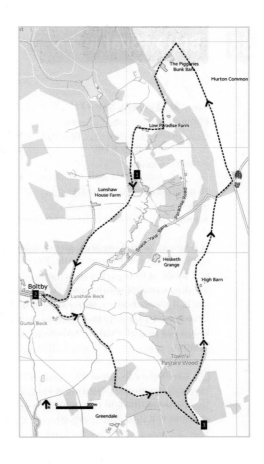

Points of interest

Boltby Scar – An important Iron Age site. As well as Boltby Scar hillfort, there is a second hillfort at Roulston Scar and defensive earthworks. There have been a number of recent archaeological excavations to try and find out about the hillfort's original construction, its subsequent defensive uses and its relationship to other features in the wider landscape.

Black Hambleton

START At SE479959, Square
Corner (on minor road between
Osmotherley and Hawnby), DL6 3QB

DISTANCE 6 miles (9.7 km)

SUMMARY An easy walk mainly along
moorland tracks, with one wet
section

PARKING Roadside parking

MAPS Explorer OL26; OS Sheets
Landranger 100

WHERE TO EAT AND DRINK None

A fine walk mostly over moorland with panoramic views.

[1] From the car park, head south along the broad stony track
heading towards Hambleton End. Ignore any tracks leading off to
the right, and keep climbing alongside the wall on the Cleveland
Way path. Eventually the climb eases and the view to the right
opens out over the Vale of Mowbray. Keep on the track until a
junction is reached at White Gill Head.

[2] Leave the Cleveland Way and go left on a track. Keep on this
through the heather, with good views down into the infant River
Rye valley on the left. On reaching a grassy area, go left, heading
down in the valley on another track. Keep left where this forks, and
keep on downhill. Leave the track where it turns sharp right and
goes through a gate, then take the path alongside the wall to reach
another gate in the valley bottom.

[3] Join a path and go left along it, aiming for a distant red roofed
barn (this section can be very wet/boggy) to reach a bridge over
a stream. Cross this and head across a field towards the ruined
house. Join a track in front of it and follow this to the left as it passes
between the buildings and then towards a plantation. Keep along
the track to eventually join a road. Go left and follow this back to
the car park.

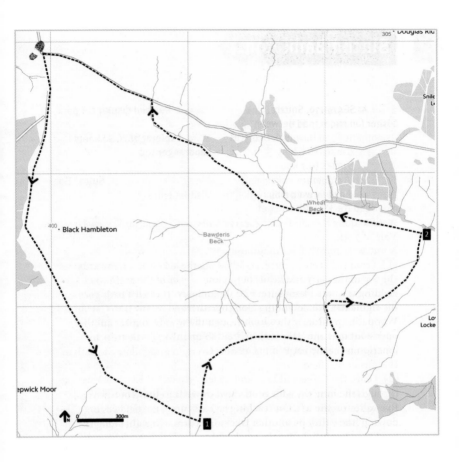

Points of interest

🔍 The Hambleton Hills – A range of hills, formed on the western edge of the North York Moors, separated by the valley of the River Rye. They are east of the Vale of Mowbray, which borders an escarpment. They run in a north-south direction for fifteen miles and merge with the Cleveland Hills (north) and Howardian Hills (south).

Sutton Bank

START At SE514829, Sutton Bank
Visitor Centre, YO7 2EH

DISTANCE 6 miles (9.6 km)

SUMMARY A moderate walk mainly
along field and forest paths

PARKING Pay and display car park

MAPS Explorer 26; OS Sheets
Landranger 100

WHERE TO EAT AND DRINK Sutton Bank
Visitor Centre

A walk along the sandstone escarpments, with panoramic views over the
Vale of York.

1 From the visitor centre, go left along the access road, towards
the top of the A170 road. Just before the corner of the main road, go
right onto a path along Sutton Brow. Follow this until a path goes
off on the left. Go downhill along this path and follow into Garbutts
Wood. The path winds its way through the woods to meet another
path. Go right onto this path and climb up through the trees to
emerge on the top edge of the woods. Go right and follow the path to
the corner of a field.

2 Go left along the edge of the field towards a clump of trees and
then go left again at these. Follow the path along the field edge,
passing horse gallops to reach Dialstone Farm. Go right along the
road here to a T-junction. Keep straight ahead into the field and
follow the path, passing Hambleton High House, over the fields to
Hambleton House. Keep ahead over more horse gallops onto a track.
Then keep right at the junction with the road, and follow this to the
junction with the A170, in front of a hotel. Go right along the main
road, passing the hotel to a road junction on the left.

3 Carefully cross the road and go along the road, signposted to the
White Horse. Follow the road, past the gliding club to parking area.

4 Leave the road and go right onto a path. Follow this to the top
of the White Horse. Keep ahead along the good track along the edge
of the escarpment, keeping an eye open for planes/gliders taking off

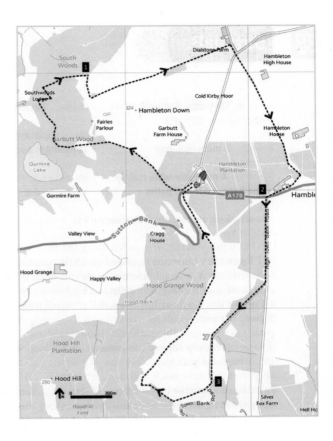

over your head. Keep on for about a mile back towards Sutton Bank, keeping right where the track forks to reach the A170. Carefully re-cross this back to the visitor centre.

Points of interest

The White Horse – The White Horse of Kilburn is one of Yorkshire's most famous landmarks, visible from thirty miles or more away. The horse is a fine viewpoint with York Minster visible, if you know where to look, on a clear day.

Baysdale

START At NZ651074, Hob Hole, YO21 2DQ

DISTANCE 6 miles (9.6 km)

SUMMARY A moderate walk, mainly on field and moorland paths

PARKING Roadside parking

MAPS Explorer 26; OS Sheets Landranger 94

WHERE TO EAT AND DRINK None

A lovely walk around the Baysdale valley.

1 From the parking area, go left along the road and climb steeply to a T-junction. Leave the road and go left along a gated track. Follow this over open moorlands for about a mile, where a wall is joined, on your left. Stay along the track following the wall, to where it makes a sharp left turn. Pass a small group of trees and then the walls turn right.

2 Go right along the wall, to where it climbs to a wall corner. Go left through the gate and follow the wall on the left over the moors. Keep over moors to reach a road, go left over the cattle grid, then leave the road almost immediately. As it turns to the right, keep straight ahead downhill towards Baysdale Abbey. Go left in front of the buildings, along a track. Keep left at the T-junction, then go right at the next junction. Follow the track into woods, and climb to the top edge of these.

3 Exit through a gate onto open moors, leave the track and go left along the wall. The path bears right away from the wall to join a track. Go left along this and follow it to where it turns sharp left, just after a track goes off on the right. Leave the track, go ahead along a path through the heather, stay on this over the moors to reach the road. Go left along the road, then left again at the junction and follow the road downhill to the car park.

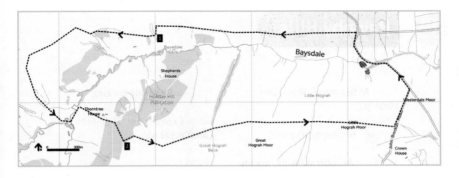

Points of interest

Westerdale – At the south-east corner of the main street is a cottage named Arkangel. The curious stone monument in the garden was erected by Thomas Bulmer, an old sailor. The lettering around the shaft relates to the many countries he had visited on his voyages and how he survived a shipwreck in 1729.

START At SE539916, Moor Gate,
YO62 5QJ

DISTANCE 6½ miles (10.5 km)

SUMMARY An easy walk, mainly on
moorland paths

PARKING Roadside parking

MAPS Explorer 26; OS Sheets
Landranger 100

WHERE TO EAT AND DRINK None

A lovely walk around two hills with fine views over Ryedale.

(1) From the parking area, head north along the track over Sunley
Slack. Where it forks keep right, then right again at the second
fork a bit further along the track. The track joins a wall briefly
before reaching Ladhill Beck.

(2) Cross the beck and keep along the track as it turns the head
of Ladhill Gill and begins to head south. Leave the track where it
starts to bear to the left, and go right along a fainter path through
the heather. Follow this to a crossroad of paths. Go right here
along a track to join a wall. Follow the wall for a while then go
through a gate. Keep ahead to reach another gate, facing you. Go
left here, through the wall and over moorland along a path. Soon a
wall appears on the right. Keep along the path as it bears round to
the right, following the wall, to approach Easterside Hill. The path
goes left alongside a wall over the lower slopes of this to reach a
corner of a small enclosed field.

(3) Go right along the wall, and then where the wall turns away
to the left, keep straight ahead, climbing over the shoulder of
Easterside Hill. The path turns south and descends steeply, then
go over a field to a road. Go right along the road and follow into
Hawnby village.

(4) Just after passing the telephone box, go right up a path
between houses. Keep left behind these, crossing a grassy area.
Climb up through trees and then keep climbing over moorland

onto Hanby Hill. Head north along its ridge, following the path, with fine views in all directions. Descend to a wall, go through a gap and keep heading north back to the parking area.

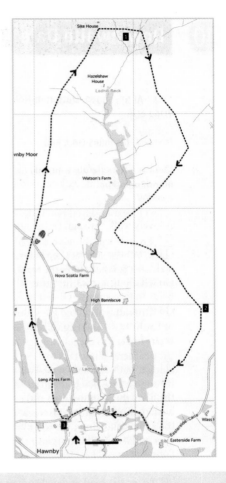

Points of interest

Hawnby – The village sits at a junction close to the B1257 road, between Oswaldkirk and Stokesley, its nearest settlements Boltby to the south-west; Old Byland to the south and Fangdale Beck to the north. Hawnby lies between Ladwith Beck and the River Rye, at an elevation of 500 feet above sea level.

START At SE705902, Hutton-le-Hole, YO62 6UA

DISTANCE 6½ miles (10.5 km)

SUMMARY A moderate walk mainly on woodland paths, with some road walking

PARKING Pay and display car park

MAPS Explorer OL26; OS Sheets Landranger 94

WHERE TO EAT AND DRINK The Crown, Hutton-le-Hole
http://crownhuttonlehole.com

A lovely walk through the wooded Dowthwaite Valley.

1 From the car park, go left along the road into the village, then right along the main road. Keep on until the last house on the left. Go left along a track just after it, through a gate, then right across fields to join a track. Go left to a gate leading onto open moors. Go through it and then left onto a track, keeping right where it forks. Keep on then go right at the next fork and descend to a footbridge.

2 Cross this and then go diagonally left over two fields, then left alongside a hedge, downhill to another footbridge. Cross this then go right to join a track, which is followed around farm buildings, on your left. Go right uphill along the farm access track, then left along a track which leads into Gillamoor village. Go straight ahead through the village, then left just after the pub. Follow the road past the play area to a footpath sign on the left.

3 Leave the road and go left over three fields, then keep right down into the woods. Follow the Shepherds Road through the woods to a fork in the track.

4 Keep left and follow the track until another junction. This time go right and follow it uphill to join a track on the edge of the woods. Go left along this and follow it to the back of Parks Road. Go left along the road and keep on to a T-junction.

5 Go left to Ravenswick. Follow the road down to houses beside a ford, and keep left to cross the footbridge over the river. Follow the track uphill to a junction with the road. Go left here and walk back along the grass verge to Hutton-le-Hole.

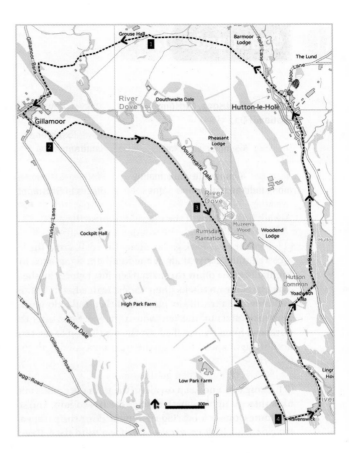

Points of interest

The Ryedale Folk Museum in Hutton-le-Hole – The museum holds numerous rescued and reconstructed historic buildings, such as an Iron Age round house, period shops, thatched cottages, an Elizabethan manor house, barns and workshops. These buildings display ordinary people's lives up to the present day. You can shop here, grab a bite to eat at the café or attend craft workshops.

Goathland

Start At NZ828052, Grosmont Station, YO22 5PA

Distance 6½ miles (10.4 km)

Summary A moderate walk mainly along field and moorland paths

Parking Pay and display car park

Maps Explorer 27; OS Sheets Landranger 94

Where to eat and drink Various places in Grosmont village

A walk linking two of the moors' famous villages.

[1] From the car park go left along the road, cross the level crossing, then go right along the footpath, signposted to the Engine Sheds. Follow this path, then just before the sheds, go right over the railways tracks, then almost immediately left. Follow the path down to the railway tracks and then walk alongside them. The tracks start to bear left away from you. Soon after this, a terrace of houses is reached. Go across the top of the terrace and keep straight ahead through the trees on a good path to reach a footbridge.

[2] Cross this and keep on along the path over fields and then back into woods. The path crosses the river again, and soon after it re-crosses it via a footbridge. Keep on along the path, passing Beck Hole on your left to cross the river for a third time. Keep ahead to join a road in Goathland.

[3] Go left to a crossroads, then right to follow the road through the village. Keep on till a broad gravel road goes off on your left. Follow this to emerge near to Goathland Station. Go left along the road to the station, and go right to cross the footbridge, then go left to join a track at the end of the platform. Follow this track alongside the railway line to a road. Go right along the road, past a house, then take the path climbing up to the left to join a track leading to another house. Pass in front of the house, and follow the track along the wall over moorland. Where the wall ends, keep on in the same direction, descending past a disused quarry to a

road. Go right along the road, pass some cottages then turn left onto the track leading to Liberty Hall. Follow this down to the farm.

4 Walk past the farm and keep right. The track turns to the right and passes between buildings. Keep straight ahead, between walls across fields. Where the path turns towards the railway line, keep right into woods. Follow the path back through Crag Cliff Wood to Grosmont village.

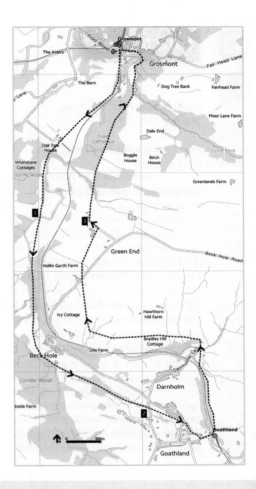

Points of interest

Goathland – The village was the setting of the fictional village, Aidensfield, in ITV's 1960s drama *Heartbeat*. There are many recognizable landmarks from the series, including the stores, garage/funeral directors, its railway station and the pub. The pub is actually called the Goathland Hotel but in *Heartbeat* it is the Aidensfield Arms.

Urra Moor

Start At NZ572035, Clay Bank, TS9 7JA

Distance 6¾ miles (10.8 km) or 8½ miles (13.7 km)

Summary Strenuous walks mainly along moorland paths

Parking Roadside car park

Maps Explorer OL26; OS Sheets Landranger 93

Where to eat and drink The Buck Inn, Chop Gate
www.the-buck-inn.co.uk

Two walks around the head of the Bilsdale valley.

1 From the car park, walk south, uphill to the top of the Chop Gate road where the Cleveland Way crosses it.

2 Cross the road and go right up the stone steps and follow the track uphill, going left over a stile to begin the steep climb up onto the flat topped Hasty Bank, and then onto the rocky outcrops of The Wainstones at the far end. Pick your way through the rocks/boulders and continue down to a gate through the wall. Climb up another steep stone pitched path to the summit of Cold Moor. At the top go left and follow the track along the long ridge of Cold Moor, heading back to Chop Gate. Ignore the cross paths, and continue until the track forks. Just after Three Howes, go left and follow it downhill to a gate in a stone wall. Go through it onto Cold Moor Lane. Follow this for a short distance downhill to a footpath sign on the left.

3 Leave the lane here and go diagonally left across the field to join a lane. Go right along this down through trees to reach the B1257 opposite a junction. Cross the road and take the minor road, signposted St Hilda's Church. Follow the lane uphill as far as Bilsdale Hall Farm. Leave the lane here and go through the gate on the right into a walled grassy lane. Keep on following the track uphill alongside the wall. Keep left where it forks to reach a gate, go through and keep going uphill to reach another gate which gives access to the open moors. Continue along the rough track uphill for about 50 metres.

4 Here, go left onto a path, which follows an ancient earthwork over the slopes of Urra Moor, which is still visible in places. The first section of this path can be wet/muddy but soon improves. The path contours the moorland to reach a stream. After crossing this, the path then turns abruptly to the north onto Carr Ridge. Keep along this until Cleveland Way is joined at a gate. Go left through this and follow the stone pitched path downhill to reach the B1257 again.

5 Go right downhill back to the car park.

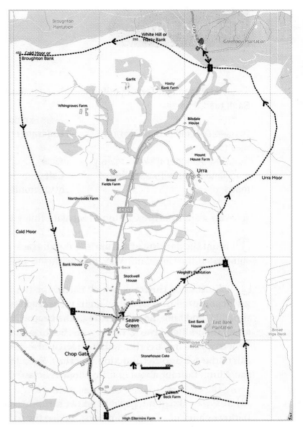

6 For the longer walk, at Cold Moor Lane, keep on along the lane and stay on this to reach Chop Gate village. At the road junction go right along the B1257. Pass the village hall and keep on along the verge to the entrance to William Hill Farm.

7 Leave the road and go left along the access track to the farm. Enter the yard, and bear right to pass the buildings, onto a grassy track on the right. Go through the gate and follow the track steeply uphill to reach a wide track on the tops of the moors. Go left along this and follow it until you are almost level with the end of East Bank Plantation. Go left here onto a rough path through the heather to a path junction near Medd Crag.

44 Carlton Moor

START At NZ522030, Top of Carlton Bank road, TS9 7JH

DISTANCE 6¾ miles (10.9 km)

SUMMARY A moderate walk mainly moorland paths with a section of roads

PARKING Roadside car park

MAPS Explorer 26; OS Sheets Landranger 93

WHERE TO EAT AND DRINK Lords Stone Café
http://lordstones.com

A lovely walk over the Carlton Moor with fine views.

① From the parking area, take the rough track heading south, signposted the Cleveland Way. Follow this to a gate.

② Climb along the track, which used to be the access road to the old glider station. Just past an old quarry, the track turns sharp right. Leave the track and take the path through the heather on the left. Continue along this, which gives great views down into Raisedale on your left. When a cross track is reached, turn left and follow this, passing a large cairn to reach another junction of tracks. Keep left again and head in the same direction for about ½ mile to reach Brian's Pond.

③ Just past the pond, go right on the signposted path heading for Barkers Crags (it's boggy in places). When the tops of the crags are reached, don't descend. Turn right and follow the path along the top of them, this gives stunning views down into Scugdale. When a stile is reached, cross it and take the path on the left, down through the crags. Keep to the left at the bottom of the crags and follow the path down over a ladder stile to reach the road at the bottom.

④ Turn right and follow the road through the Scugdale valley for a couple of miles. Even though it's all on tarmac, it's still a delightful walk, until Huthwaite Green is reached.

⑤ Go right through the wooden gate at Huthwaite Green onto a path through the woods. At first the climbing is easy, however, this doesn't

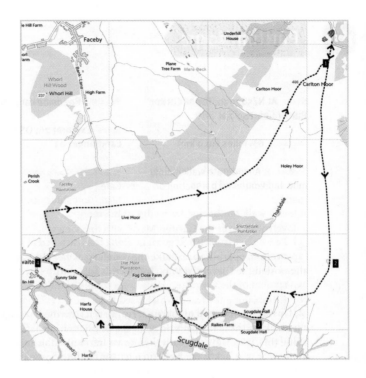

last. There is a steep pull up Knolls End to reach the stile at the top where you exit the woods and head back out onto open moors. The going is much easier now and there's a good path over Live Moor and Faceby Bank to reach the trig point on Carlton Bank. From the trig point, go right downhill along the stone pitched path, which is steep in places, to reach the gate.

6 Turn left to reach the road/parking area.

Points of interest

Lords Stones – Just to the north of the café, there is a small stone circle and some large standing stones.

45 Pinchinthorpe

START At NZ583152, Pinchinthorpe
Visitor Centre, TS14 8HD

DISTANCE 6¾ miles (10.9 km)

SUMMARY An easy walk, mainly on
field and woodland paths

PARKING Pay and display car park

MAPS Explorer 26; OS Sheets
Landranger 93

WHERE TO EAT AND DRINK None

A lovely walk on the northern edge of the moors.

1 Leave the car park and go right along the track bed of the old
railway line, now a walking and cycling route. Cross the road and keep
ahead along the old railway. Follow it over fields, with fine views of the
escarpment of the Cleveland Hills, for a couple of miles.

2 Just before the end of the walkway, go left into the fields and follow
a path along the left edge. Briefly walk alongside the Middlesbrough to
Whitby railway way. The path then bears left across the field to cross a
footbridge over a stream. Keep on over the fields to Snow Hall Farm,
enter the yard and go left between the buildings. Then keep right at
the end of them to join the farm access track, which leads to the road
junction in Newton under Roseberry.

3 Go right along the road, past the pub, then go left onto Roseberry
Lane. Follow this uphill towards Roseberry Topping, at the top of the
lane go through a gate into the woods. Go left and follow the path
through the trees. At a gate go steeply up to the right to a stile. Cross this
and keep climbing along Brant Gate. Where the path forks keep right,
keep ahead, ignore paths on the left and keep on to reach a broad track.
Go right along this and follow it into woods. Ignore the track going off
on the right and keep ahead to a four-way junction of tracks.

4 Go left, almost doubling back on yourself and follow the track as it
winds its way through the trees. At a junction on the edge of the woods,
keep left to join the old railway line. Go left along this back to the car
park.

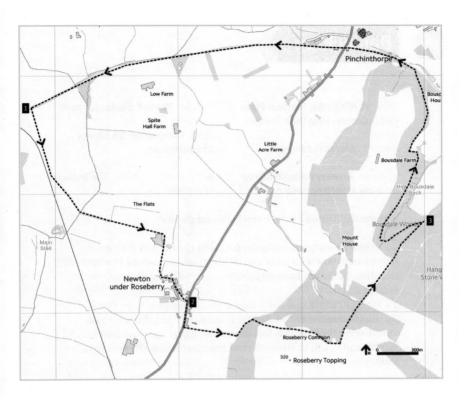

Points of interest

Roseberry Topping – The summit has a distinctive half-cone shape with a jagged cliff, and has often been compared to the Matterhorn in Switzerland. Roseberry Topping was thought to be the highest hill on the North York Moors at 1,049 feet but Urra Moor is higher, at 1,490 feet. Views of Captain Cook's Monument at Easby Moor and the monument at Eston Nab can be seen from here.

START At NZ717083, National Park Visitor Centre in Danby, YO21 2NB

DISTANCE 7 miles (11.2 km)

SUMMARY A moderate walk mainly along field and moorland paths

PARKING Pay and display car park

MAPS Explorer 26; OS Sheets Landranger 94

WHERE TO EAT AND DRINK The National Park Visitor Centre

A fine walk visiting Little Fryup Dale and Danby Rigg.

1 From the car park, cross the road and go through the gate onto a footpath. Follow this over fields, cross the railway line and keep ahead to reach Easton Lane.

2 Go right along this and follow it to Ainthorpe village. Cross the bridge, then at the T-junction, go left, then go left onto Brook Lane. Keep left where this forks, continue along the road, past the pub and uphill to where the road turns left, just after a tennis court.

3 Leave the road here and go right onto a track, which climbs over Ainthorpe Rigg to the edge of the escarpment. Don't descend, go right along the edge, crossing a track near to the trig point. Keep on along the edge of Danby Rigg, ignoring any cross paths to reach the road.

4 Go right along a track descending on the left. Leave the road and follow the track down into fields, cross these to another road. Go left along the road to Stonebeck Gate Farm, going right just before the buildings onto a track. Follow this as far as Forester's Lodge. Leave the track and go diagonally right past the buildings, to a gate. Go through this, along a short section of walled lane, then left across the field to another wall lane. At the end, go through a gate and keep ahead to reach the road.

5 Go right along Castle Lane to Danby Castle. Go right at the junction, and follow the road to another junction at Duck Bridge. Keep left here and follow the road back to Easton Lane.

6 Go right and retrace your route back to the car park.

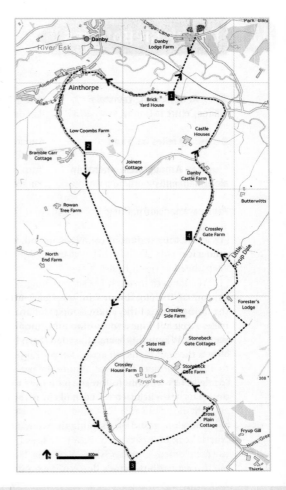

Points of interest

Danby Rigg – The site of a Bronze Age settlement, by over 300 small cairns. A standing stone is the sole survivor of a 42 feet diameter stone circle. At its centre two urn burials, dating back to 1000 BC, were excavated.

47 Levisham Bottoms

START At SE833905, Levisham village, YO18 7NL

DISTANCE 7 miles (11.2 km)

SUMMARY An easy walk, mainly on moorland paths

PARKING Roadside parking

MAPS Explorer 27; OS Sheets Landranger 94

WHERE TO EAT AND DRINK The Horseshoe Inn, Levisham http://www.horseshoelevisham. co.uk

An interesting walk that combines legend, history and spectacular scenery.

[1] Walk north through Levisham village. Where the road forks in front of The Horseshoe Inn, keep left onto Braygate Lane. Follow this and where it forks again, keep right and keep on for about a mile. Leave the lane and go onto open moors, following the wall on your left. Where this turns sharp left, turn left and keep following. When the wall turns left again, keep straight ahead a short distance to a path junction. Go right, ignore the path going off almost immediately left, and follow the path over the moors, before it descends, then bear left to reach Skelton Tower.

[2] There are grand views along the wooded valley below and the North York Moors railway. From the tower, go east along the edge of the escarpment onto Levisham Bottoms. Stay on the path as it heads north-east, with the steep slopes of Wet Side Brow on your right. Stay on this path for a couple of miles, where it forks keep right to reach a hair pin bend on the A169.

[3] Join a track here and go right along, climbing up onto Gallows Dyke, with fine views down into the Hole of Horcum. Stay on the track over Levisham Moor, to reach Dundale Pond. Go diagonally left at the pond to soon reach a gate leading into a walled lane. Go along this lane and follow it back into Levisham village, keeping left at the pub back to the start.

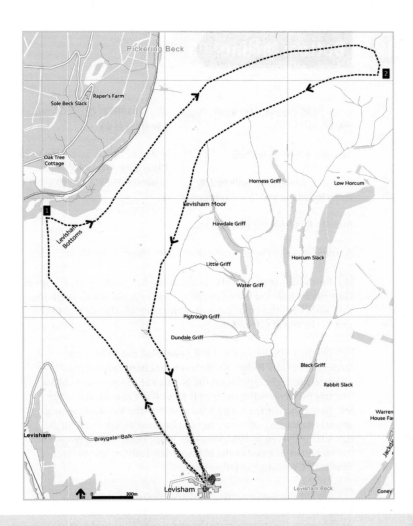

Points of interest

Skelton Tower – Originally a shooting lodge, it was built by Reverend Robert Skelton, Rector of Levisham, in the first part of the nineteenth century.

Bottom Incline

START At NZ572035, Clay Bank, TS9 7JA

DISTANCE 7½ miles (12 km)

SUMMARY A moderate walk mainly along moorland and forest tracks

PARKING Roadside car park

MAPS Explorer OL26; OS Sheets Landranger 93

WHERE TO EAT AND DRINK The Buck Inn, Chop Gate
www.the-buck-inn.co.uk

A fine walk over the highest point on the North York Moors.

1 From the car park, walk south, uphill to the top of the Chop Gate road where the Cleveland Way crosses it. Go left through the gate and climb the stone pitched path alongside the wall up to the gate at the top of Carr Ridge.

2 Go through the gate and keep ahead on the wide track leading over Carr Ridge. At the track junction, keep left and climb to the highest point on the North York Moors, Urra Moor. The trig point marking the spot is just off the main track to the left. Return to the track and head east over the moors, ignoring any tracks leading off to the right. Also keep an eye open for interesting carved stones along the side of the track. Keep on to reach the track bed of the old Rosedale railway, just before Bloworth Crossing. Go left to join it.

3 Go left through a cutting and keep on to the incline top. You will pass a bench along the way, which provides a great viewpoint. At the top of the incline, pass the remains of the building that was used to haul the trucks up and down the slope. Going down the incline is much easier than going up it – regardless of which way you do it, it's still an impressive sight and would have been even more impressive with the ore laden trucks descending. At the bottom, enter woods to reach a track junction.

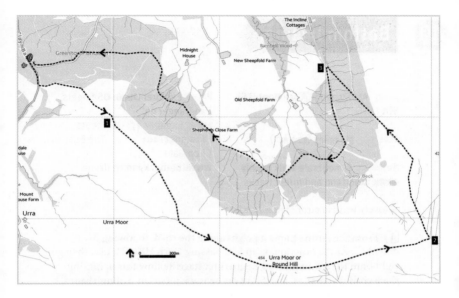

(4) Go left along the track through the woods, which winds its way around the head of the valley. Ignore the track leading off to the right, and then keep right at the first fork. Keep on through the trees to a second fork in the track. This time keep left and stay along this track to reach a road. Go left along it and climb up through the trees to the car park.

Points of interest

Botton Incline – The railway to Rosedale was built in 1861 to transport the iron ore to the furnaces in Teesside. The incline allowed the trucks to be raised/lowered from the valley floor to the tops of the moors at over 1,300 feet. There was a drum house at the top, the remains of which can still be seen. The incline runs for 1 mile, in which it climbs 750 vertical feet.

Basin Howe

START At SE913868, Cockmoor Hall, YO13 9EG

DISTANCE 7¾ miles (12.5 km)

SUMMARY A moderate walk mainly along forest tracks/paths

PARKING Roadside parking

MAPS Explorer 27; OS Sheets Landranger 101

WHERE TO EAT AND DRINK None

A lovely walk around Trouts Dale.

[1] From the parking area go right along the road, following it downhill. At the junction, keep left, passing Hern Head House, then go right onto a track in front of Keepers Cottage. Follow this uphill into the woods, keeping straight over at the track junction. Follow the track over Troutsdale moor for about a mile, until just after a track comes in diagonally from the left.

[2] Leave the track and go right over moorland, along the edge of trees. Keep on in the same direction to the edge of the moors. Go diagonally left down through woods to Troutsdale Lodge. Go to the right of this to join a road. Go left along the road for a short distance. Go right along a track, go over two fields, then turn left along a hedge and follow the path uphill into woods. The path climbs steeply through the trees to a forest track.

[3] Go left along the track and follow it for about 1 mile to a junction. Go right onto Moors Road and follow this, ignoring the track going off on the right. Then keep right where the track forks to climb up to the road on Highwood Brow.

[4] Go right along the road for about ¼ mile, then go left onto a track. Follow this, taking the first track off on the right. Keep straight ahead along this track for about a mile, ignoring any tracks leading off to the left or right to reach a road. Go right along this, to the entrance of Basin Howe cottages. Leave the road and take the track along the edge of the woods, then turn left at the corner of the woods and follow the track back to the parking area.

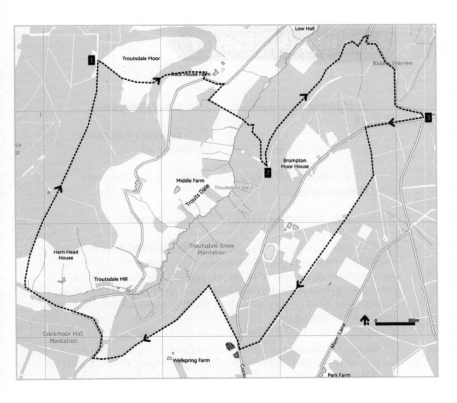

Points of interest

Basin Howe – A fairly large example of a howe, or burial mound. Unfortunately it cannot be visited. The are many other earthworks in the area, including The Three Tremblers.

50 The Quakers Causeway

START At NZ658148, Birks Brow,
TS12 3LD

DISTANCE 7¾ miles (12.5 km)

SUMMARY A moderate walk mainly
along moorland paths

PARKING Roadside parking

MAPS Explorer 26; OS Sheets
Landranger 90

WHERE TO EAT AND DRINK None

A fine walk over the moors along ancient stone pathways.

1 Facing the A171, leave the car park by the left hand exit.
Carefully cross the busy road, onto a track opposite. Follow this
south over the moors, to a junction of paths on Woodhill Gill
Head. Go left here and follow the path south to a track, near to
grouse butts. Go straight ahead along this for a short distance,
leaving it by keeping ahead where the track turns right. Keep
ahead for about ¼ mile until a path joins from the right.

2 Go left at the junction and follow the path south-east over
the moors for about 1 mile. Walk along Smeathorns Road just
briefly, go right along it and then take the path downhill, where
the road turns away. Follow the path downhill to reach another
road.

3 Go right along the road and follow into Commondale
village. Keep right past the pub at the junction, and follow the
road uphill past houses. At the end of the houses, leave the road
and go right onto open moorland. Keep on to a path that joins
from the left, then descend to the right to cross a stream via a
footbridge. Climb up the bank on the opposite side and follow
the path through the heather. Keep ahead to join a track coming
up from North Ings. Go right along this and follow it until it
turns to the left, and a path goes off on the right.

4 Go right along the path and head north. Keep on for about
1 mile to reach a wall, and cross a path. Go right along the path,

following the wall for a short distance. Keep on as the path bears away from the wall to reach High Moor.

5 Go left and retrace your outward route back to the car park.

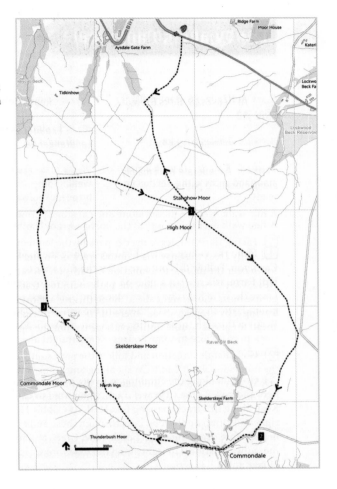

The Quakers Causeway – One of the many stone flagged trods that cross the moors. It runs from White Cross, just to the East of Commondale over the moors to Guisborough.

Danby and Commondale

START At NZ707086, Danby village,
YO21 2LY

DISTANCE 8 miles (12.9 km)

SUMMARY A moderate walk mainly
moorland paths with a section on
roads

PARKING Limited roadside car parking

MAPS Explorer 26; OS Sheets
Landranger 94

WHERE TO EAT AND DRINK The Duke of
Wellington
http://dukeofwellingtondanby.co.uk

A fine walk over the moors to the north-west of Danby.

1 From the village centre, head west along the road to
Castleton. Follow this until just after the entrance to Winsley
Hill Farm, where a track goes off to the left over open ground.
Leave the road here and go left along the track, first over open
ground, which can be wet, then into the woods of Danby Park.
Keep on through these, exiting via a gate, then ahead along the
track to pass close to some houses. Keep straight ahead to reach
a road.

2 Go right along the climbing to where it turns. Leave the road
here and go left along a gravel track, signposted to Commondale.
Keep along this track, passing Box Hall. At Cobble Hall, keep
right and climb up to trees. Pass through these and then on over
fields before dropping down beside Fowl Green to a road near to
the railway station. Go right along the road into Commondale
village and a T-junction.

3 Go right at the junction and climb along the road out of the
village. It's steep at first, but soon levels out. Continue along the
road to another T-junction on Three Howes Rigg. Cross the road
and go straight ahead along a sandy track. Follow this over Haw
Rigg, then descend slightly over a wet area, then climb again
onto Siss Cross Hill. Keep on until a rough track comes in from
the left. Soon after this a marker post on the right is reached.

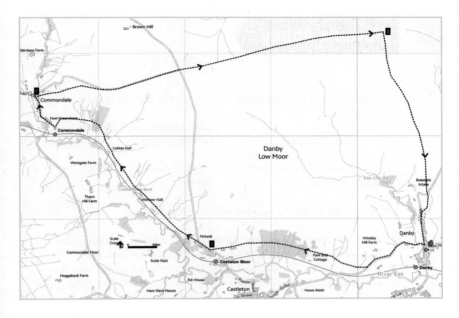

4 Go right along a peaty path through the heather, which can be wet in places. Follow this over Danby Low Moor. After passing a cairn, which gives great views over Danby Dale, the path descends gently down towards Danby. It can be very muddy in places, but the road is soon reached. Go right along it and follow it downhill back into the village.

Points of interest

Flagged Causeways – These are typical of many to be found on the North York Moors. Many of the routes can be traced back to medieval times and may have been pioneered by monks on the routes between abbeys and granges. These causeways were at one time the only means of communication across the moors.

WALK

52 Rievaulx Abbey

START At SE574849, Rievaulx Abbey, YO62 5LB

DISTANCE 8 miles (12.9 km)

SUMMARY A moderate walk mainly on woodland paths

PARKING Pay and display car park

MAPS Explorer 26; OS Sheets Landranger 100

WHERE TO EAT AND DRINK Rievaulx Abbey

A lovely walk around the wooded valleys of Ryedale.

1 From the car park, go left along the road and follow it to Rievaulx Bridge. Go right over the bridge and follow the road to a junction. Keep left and follow the road past Hagg Hall to where it enters woods. Leave the road and go right, through gates into the woods. Go along the track, with ponds on the right to a junction of tracks.

2 Keep straight ahead a short distance, then go right at the next junction and follow the track along the edge of the woods. At the next junction, keep right and stay on the path through the bottom of Nettle Dale Wood. Ignore the track coming down from the left, and keep on to where the track forks. Go right into Tanker Dale and follow the track to join a road.

3 Go right along the road into Old Byland, and go left at the first junction. Keep ahead, ignoring the roads going off on both sides to where the road turns sharp left and starts to descend. Keep on down the road to a bridleway sign on the right. Go right here over fields to enter woods. Keep on ahead through the woods for about 1 mile to a track junction near to Tylas Farm. Go straight across and follow the track over fields into the woods. Keep on till the track descends to a cross path junction on the edge of the trees.

4 Cross the field ahead along a track, then over the River Rye on Bow Bridge. The track then bears to the right, stay on it through the woods to reach the road. Go right along the road back to the car park.

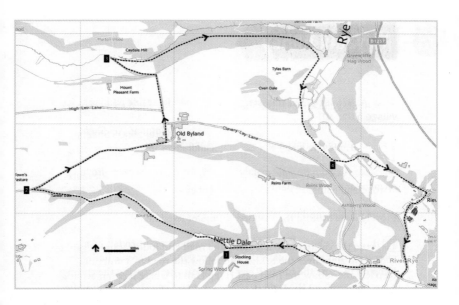

Points of interest

Rievaulx Abbey – The first large Cistercian church to be built in England. The ruins and village are set in a beautiful valley. Rievaulx Terrace, set above the abbey, has half a mile of lawn and two classical temples.

Westerdale ▶

START At NZ664058, Westerdale
village, YO21 2DT

DISTANCE 8¼ miles (13.3 km)

SUMMARY A moderate walk mainly
on moorland and field paths

PARKING Roadside parking

MAPS Explorer 26; OS Sheets
Landranger 94

WHERE TO EAT AND DRINK None

A fine walk around the Westerdale valley.

1 From the church, go right along the road, then turn left just
after the village hall. Follow downhill, passing Westerdale hall.
Keep on to cross the infant River Esk. Soon after crossing the river,
a track goes off on the right to Grange Farm. Keep straight ahead to
reach the wall on the edge of the moors. Go through the gate and
follow the track, left, along the edge of the moors to New House
Farm. Just before the farm, go left into fields. Keep ahead along a
path, cross a track to Hill House. Then pass to the right of Wood
End. Keep along trees on your left to cross another track.

2 Cross this and then cross the stream, turn right and follow the
stream. Keep on over three fields, then exit onto open moorland.
Keep ahead along a path, still following the infant River Esk
upstream. Enter a wall enclosure to join a track. Go left along this to
a T-junction.

3 Go left along the track to where it crosses the stream, leave it
and go right following the wall. Keep along the path as it climbs,
passing grouse butts, to reach the road. Go straight across and keep
on along the path across the head of the Rosedale valley to another
road.

4 Go straight over, follow the path through the heather to the
road. Cross this and take the path downhill, passing grouse butts.
Keep to the right walls in the valley bottom; follow these round to
reach Dale Head.

5 Pass to the left of the buildings, on a path, keep along this over fields, cross a stream to reach Broad Gate Farm. Go through the yard onto a road, keep straight ahead on this back towards Westerdale village. Ignore the track going off on the right, and keep onto crossroads. Go left to a T-junction, then right back to the start.

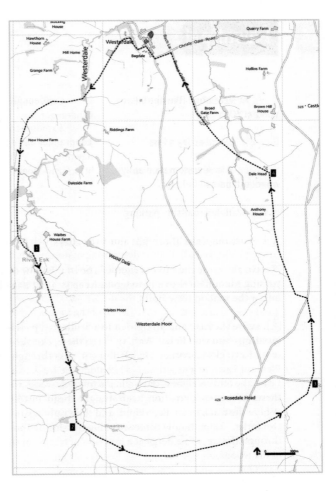

Points of interest

Moorland Crosses – There are more than twenty stone crosses to be found on the North York Moors. Many of these are on ancient routes, often erected by the religious houses in medieval times.

START At SE542897, Hawnby village, YO62 5QS

MAPS Explorer 26; OS Sheets Landranger 100

DISTANCE 8¼ miles (13.3 km)

SUMMARY A long walk mainly on woodland paths

PARKING Limited roadside parking

WHERE TO EAT AND DRINK The Inn at Hawnby http://www.innathawnby.co.uk

A walk through the Thorodale and Rye valleys.

① Go along the road to the right of The Inn. Follow this downhill, passing Manor Farm to a crossroads. Keep straight ahead and follow the road to New Hall.

② Leave the road and go right onto a bridleway, pass between buildings into woodland. Walk through these, exit the far side to join a track at a corner. Go left along it, pass through Mount Pleasant Farm to a junction. Go left along the track to a large tree. Leave the and go right over two fields towards woodlands. Enter these. At the track junction, keep straight ahead, heading west. Where the track forks, keep right, and then right again at the next two forks. The path now contours along the side of Thorodale through the trees to emerge at a junction of tracks on the top edge of the woods.

③ Go left along the track, keep ahead when a track comes in from the left. Cross the stream, then climb steeply to the corner of a wall. Go along this, heading west to join a cross track on the tops of the moors. Go left along this to where a road comes in from the right. At the crossroads, go left and descend over the moors. Enter fields and keep on gently downhill to a track junction on the edge of the woods.

④ Keep left to enter the woods, descend through the trees. Keep

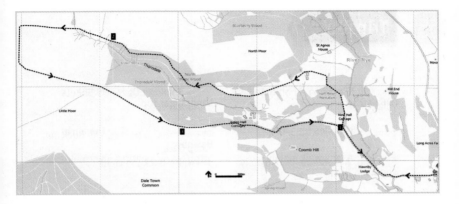

right at the next track junction to reach the road at Arden Hall. Go right along the road and follow it to New Hall.

⑤ Retrace outward route back to Hawnby village.

Points of interest

Hawnby – The village sits at a junction close to the B1257 road, between Oswaldkirk and Stokesley, its nearest settlements are Boltby to the south-west; Old Byland to the south and Fangdale Beck to the north. Hawnby lies between Ladwith Beck and the River Rye, at an elevation of 500 feet above sea level.

55 Tripsdale

Start **At SE559993, Chop Gate village hall, TS9 7JL**

Distance **8½ miles (13.7 km)**

Summary **A moderate walk mainly along moorland tracks**

Parking **Roadside car park**

Maps **Explorer OL26; OS Sheets Landranger 93**

Where to eat and drink **The Buck Inn, Chop Gate**
www.the-buck-inn.co.uk

A walk over the highest point on the North York Moors, with fine views.

[1] Leave the car park and go right along the B1257 as far as the entrance to William Beck Farm. Leave the road here and follow the track to the farm. Enter the yard, pass to the right of the building, and keep right onto a walled lane. Follow this, then continue in the same direction across the field to the open moorland. Follow the track uphill to a vehicle track on the tops of the moors.

[2] Go right along this, and then left at the next junction. Follow the track as it zig zags down into Tripsdale, cross the stream and climb back up the other side of the valley. As the ascent eases, some grouse butts are reached. Ignore the track going off on the right, and then just after keep left where the track forks. Keep on this track to reach another track junction.

[3] Go left at this junction and follow the track over the moors. Shortly after fording Badger Gill, a four way track junction is reached. Go left again and follow the track onto Cockayne Head where the Cleveland Way is joined. Go left and follow this over the moors to Round Hill, the highest point on the North York Moors. The trig point is off the track to the right. Just after this the track forks.

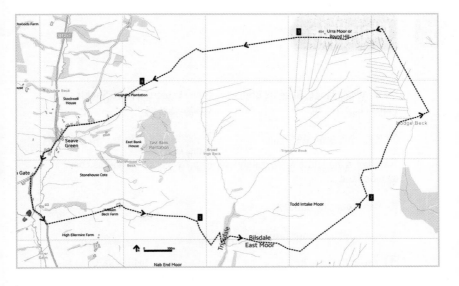

4 Keep left, and descend towards Medd Crag, to reach a gate in the wall, overlooking Bilsdale. Go through the gate and follow the track winding down to Bilsdale Hall where a road is joined. Go left along the road and follow into Seave Green. At the junction with B1257, go left and follow it back to the village hall.

Points of interest

Botton Incline – The railway to Rosedale was built in 1861 to transport the iron ore to the furnaces in Teesside. The incline allowed the trucks to be raised/lowered from the valley floor to the tops of the moors at over 1,300 feet. There was a drum house at the top, the remains of which can still be seen. The incline runs for 1 mile, in which it climbs 750 vertical feet.

56 Glaisdale

STARTAt NZ783054, Beggars Bridge, Glaisdale, YO21 2QL

DISTANCE 8¾ miles (14 km)

SUMMARY A moderate walk, mainly on moorland paths

PARKING Roadside parking

MAPS Explorer 27; OS Sheets Landranger 94

WHERE TO EAT AND DRINK The Arncliffe Arms, Glaisdale http://www.arncliffearms.com

A grand upland moor ramble.

1 From Beggars Bridge, go left under the railway bridge and follow the road towards Glaisdale village. Go right at the first road, signposted local traffic only. Follow this to reach the houses, keep right and climb steeply to reach a road junction. Go right along High Street and keep climbing to the junction with Glaisdale Hall Lane. Go left along this and follow it to its end. Keep straight ahead, along a good track over the heather moorlands of Glaisdale Moor. Where the track forks, keep left to reach the road, next to a trig point.

2 Just before the road, take the path on the left, descending into the valley. Follow this to a wall, go right along the wall to a gate. Go through this and keep left down across two fields to reach another road. Go right then immediately left to pass Yew Grange Farm. Keep on along the road to where it makes a U-turn around Mountain Ash Farm. Leave the road here and go right, uphill, and follow the winding path to Wintergill.

3 Go left along the road and follow it for roughly 3 miles over the moors. Go left at the T-junction and follow the lane, past houses, then into woods. Keep right at the junction to reach the road. Go right back to Beggars Bridge.

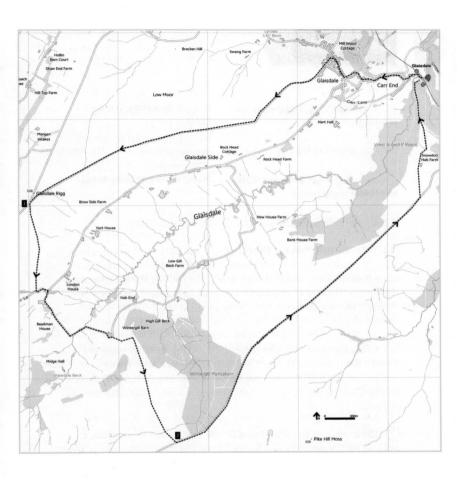

Points of interest

The Green – Despite being marked on the map as The Green, it's not typical of village greens in this area, rather, a triangular shaped area of grass.

WALK

57   Reasty Bank

START **At SE964944, Reasty Bank, YO13 0LE**

DISTANCE **8¾ miles (14 km)**

SUMMARY **A difficult walk, mainly on forest paths and tracks**

PARKING **Roadside parking**

MAPS **Explorer 27; OS Sheets Landranger 101**

WHERE TO EAT AND DRINK **None**

A hilly walk through the woodlands of the Broxa Forest.

① Take the path leaving the rear of the car park. Follow this along Surgate Brow to reach a crossroads. Go right along the road then leave it again along the path on the left. Keep along the path through the woods. It loops a couple of times back to the road, but keep on through the woods to reach the road again at the T-junction on Cumboots Brow.

② Cross the road and take the track, heading west, through the woods. Keep on over the field beyond, and at the fence corner, turn left and follow the path down through the woods into Thirsley Bottoms, where the road is joined. Go right along the road to the church and school.

③ Keep left over the bridge and follow the road to where a track goes off on the right. Leave the road here and climb through the trees, keeping right at the fork up onto Hackness Head. Exit the woods and go left, then keep right where the woods on your right go away from you. Follow the edge of these towards Broxa. Just before the houses at the end of the woods, join a track, going right along this, downhill between trees to a road. Go left along the road to Lowdales Farm.

④ Keep right, passing between the buildings into Low Dale. Follow the track through the valley bottom for about 1½ miles to Whisperdale Farm. At the junction in front of the farm, go right to shortly enter the forest. Keep on through the trees. At the junction go right, heading north-east and follow the track back to the car park.

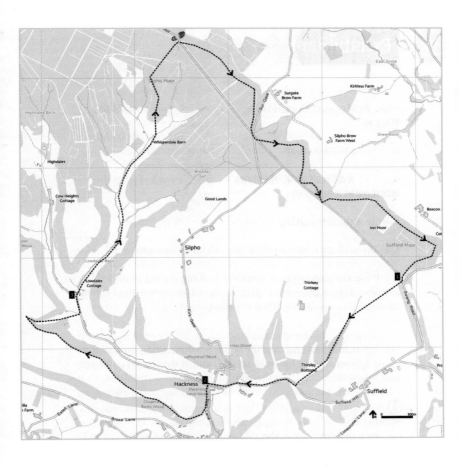

Points of interest

Hackness Hall – Located in a beautiful setting, the home of Lord Derwent. Herons are amongst the birds often seen around the lake.

START At SE659927, Rudland Rigg, YO62 7JJ

DISTANCE 9 miles (14 km)

SUMMARY A difficult walk, mainly on moorland and field paths

PARKING Roadside parking

MAPS Explorer 26; OS Sheets Landranger 100

WHERE TO EAT AND DRINK The Feversham Arms http://www.fevershamarmsinn.co.uk

A lovely walk around Farndale, famous for its daffodils.

1 From the parking area, head north along the track onto Rudland Rigg. Keep on to a track going off on the left, then shortly afterwards to one going off on the right.

2 Keep straight ahead at the junction, and follow the track north over the heather moors. Stay on in the same direction for about 3 miles. Ignore any tracks going on the sides, until you arrive at a crossroads.

3 Go right here and follow the track to a track junction, above Monket House Crags. Keep left and descend steeply to reach a road. Go right along it, then at the T-junction go left and follow the road, over Thorn Wath Bridge, to Church Houses.

4 Take the first road on the right and follow this to High Mill. Go to the right of the building and through the yard onto a path at the far side. This path is part of the Daffodil Walk, which crosses the fields along the banks of the River Dove. Follow this downstream to the car park at Low Mill.

5 Exit the car park and go left along Mill Lane. Follow this uphill to where it turns sharp left. Leave the road, and go to the right of the building ahead. Cross the field to a lane. Go straight across this, then go diagonally right across the field to enter woods. Climb up

through these, at the top go diagonally left. Climb steeply, passing disused quarries, keeping right where the path splits. Keep on over the moors to reach a track, go left along it back to Rudland Rigg.

6 Go left and walk back to the parking area.

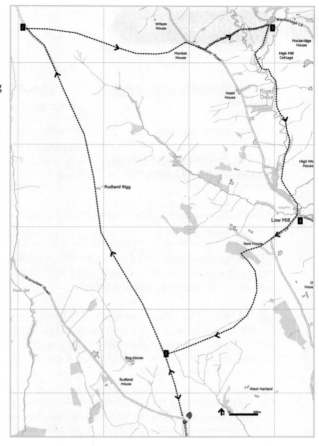

Points of interest

Farndale – Sometimes referred as Daffodil Dale because of the wild daffodils that grow in the valley in such large numbers. In the spring months, the fields along the banks of the River Dove are filled with masses of yellow daffodils.

START At SE705902, Hutton-le-Hole, YO62 6UA

DISTANCE 9 miles (14.5 km)

SUMMARY A difficult walk mainly on moorland paths, with some road walking

PARKING Pay and display car park

MAPS Explorer OL26; OS Sheets Landranger 94

WHERE TO EAT AND DRINK The Crown, Hutton-le-Hole
http://crownhuttonlehole.com

A fine walk over the heather moorlands on the south of the moors.

① From the car park, go right along Moor Road. Leave it where it turns right, and keep ahead onto a moorland track, Lodge Road. Follow this for about a mile, then where it forks keep right and continue over the moors to a T-junction.

② Go right along a track and follow it to reach the Rosedale Road. Go left along it to the top of the steep, 'Rosedale Chimney'. Descend the road a short distance, then leave it and go right down over rough ground. At the bottom keep left to rejoin the road. Go right along to a junction opposite the hotel.

③ Go right through the hotel car park, keep along the track to reach Hollins Farm. Just before the buildings, go right onto a moorland path. Climb steeply, at the junction go right and keep climbing over the moors. At the cross junction of tracks, go straight over, passing grouse butts. Keep along this track which bears to the left and then heads south over Lastingham Ridge towards Lastingham.

④ Just before the village, go right along the edge of the moors, following the wall. Keep following this to join a road. Go right along the road, stay on it until walls appear on both sides. Leave it shortly afterwards by going left over rough ground to shortly enter woods. Cross Fairy Call Beck via a footbridge, then cross four fields back into Hutton-le-Hole village. Go right along the main street back to the car park.

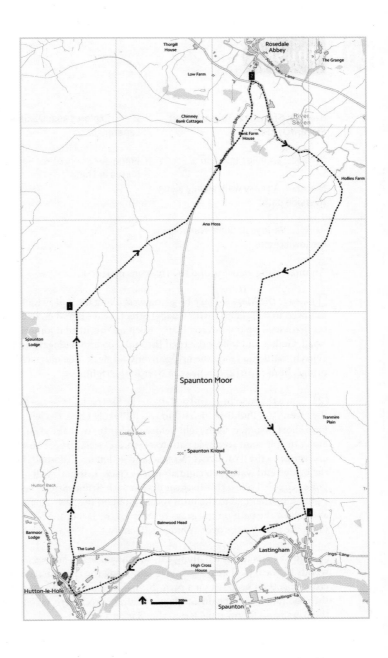

START At SE431822, Thirsk Market Place, YO7 1PL

DISTANCE 3¼ miles (5.2 km)

SUMMARY An easy walk mainly along riverside paths

PARKING Various parking available in the town centre

MAPS Explorer 302; OS Sheets Landranger 99

WHERE TO EAT AND DRINK Various places in Thirsk

An interesting walk around the environs of Thirsk.

1 Leave the Market Place by going west along the A61, which is followed to its junction with Chapel Street. Leave it and go left onto the footpath leading to Sowerby Flatts. Keep on this until it joins Sowerby Road. Go left and follow the road through Sowerby village, passing the church, until you reach the bridge over Cod Beck. The old packhorse bridge, built in 1672, can be seen over to the right.

2 Leave the road here and go left on the footpath along the banks of the river. Pass Pudding Pie Hill to reach Blakely Lane. Go left along this for a short distance, then right before the bridge over the river. Keep along the pleasant riverside path to reach the overskirts of Thirsk, to emerge onto the A61. Cross the road and go left on a footpath between the bridge and wall, then right along the river. This path will join St James Green. Follow this to the junction with Bridge Street, keeping right along the road to the mini roundabout on the A61. Turn left here and follow the path on the grass verge until the last of the houses. Keep on to the road bridge over Whiteless Beck.

3 Don't cross it. Go left along a footpath beside the houses then into woods to reach Cod Beck again. Go left, along the river to a footbridge, cross this, then keep left on a path through the woods and play area to the road junction opposite St Mary's Church. From here, go left along the B1448 and follow it back into the Market Place.

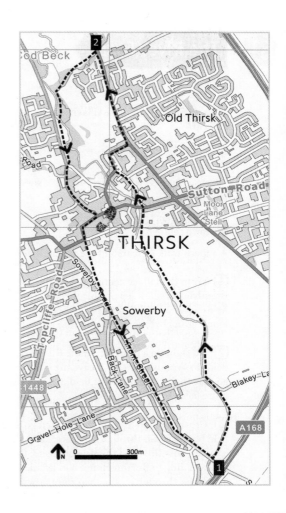

Points of interest

 Thirsk – Well known as a horse-racing town, and lesser known as the home of James Herriot the vet. There is a visitor centre in the town centre dedicated to him.

61 The River Foss

START At SE561705, Crayke village, YO61 4TA

MAPS Explorer 299; OS Sheets Landranger 100

DISTANCE 5 miles (8 km)

SUMMARY An easy walk mainly along field paths

WHERE TO EAT AND DRINK The Durham Ox, Crayke www.thedurhamox.com

PARKING Roadside parking

A superb walk in search of the young River Foss.

[1] From the village centre, go left in front of the pub and head along Brandsby Street. Keep on this through the village and then between fields as far as Mill Green Farm. Leave the road here, going left along the lane leading to Crayke Manor, into the yard.

[2] Go right on a track, cross the River Foss, keep along the track over fields to Woodfield Farm. Leave the track in front of the vast barns and go diagonally right over the field. Cross a stile, keeping ahead over two more fields to Beckfield House.

[3] Cross the road leading to and then go diagonally left across the field beside it. Go through the trees, keep ahead over the next field to a road. Cross this, and the stile opposite, then cross the field to join a track leading to Burton House. Go left along this, pass to the left of the buildings, through a gate, then right down the field to meet the River Foss in the trees. Cross the stream and follow it downstream, crossing it again, to a bridge. Cross the stream via the bridge and then uphill through the fields to reach a road. Go right along this to a footpath sign on the left.

[4] Go left through the gate, cross the field to Close House, pass through the yard. Keep heading south across fields. Cross Myra Bank Lane, keep in the same direction over fields to cross a second lane. Bear slightly right along the hedge to cross a stream via a footbridge.

⑤ Keep on in the same direction uphill. To reach the corner of the field, go left diagonally across the field to join a lane in the trees. Go right along this to the churchyard. Pass beside the church to the road, and go left along this back into the village.

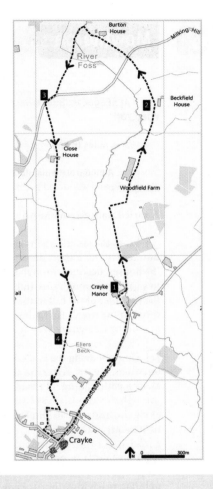

Points of interest

River Foss – The spring of this river, which is 19.5 miles in length, is situated in the Howardian Hills, above the Oulston Reservoir. The river flows in a southerly direction for most of its course towards York, where it joins the River Ouse. The river is now navigable for only 1.5 miles upstream of Castle Mills Lock.

Mowthorpe

START At SE696675, Bulmer village, YO60 7BN

DISTANCE 5 miles (8 km)

SUMMARY A moderate walk mainly along field and woodland paths

PARKING Roadside parking

MAPS Explorer 302; OS Sheets Landranger 99

WHERE TO EAT AND DRINK None

A varied walk around Mowthorpe Dale.

[1] From the junction of Wandales Lane and Bulmer Hill, go along Bulmer Hill for a short distance, then right along the lane between the houses, descend through fields to cross a stream. Then climb to a gate, go through this and follow the hedge on the left over the shoulder of the hill to the edge of Ox Pasture Wood. Descend through the woods to reach some fishing lakes, keep left past these to join the Centenary Way at a fence corner.

[2] Go right along the track, keep left onto a track leading to farm buildings. Go left in front of these, then almost immediately right along a path leading into the trees behind them. Follow the path through the woods, cross a stream, uphill to exit the woods, keeping along the field edge to join Sleigh Lane. Go left along this to where it turns sharp right.

[3] Leave the lane, going left along the field edge. Follow this around to cross a stream, turning right to follow a small valley uphill to reach Mowthorpe Lane, go left along this to the junction leading to Mowthorpe Hill Farm.

[4] Go right along the track towards the buildings, passing to the right of them to edge of Mowthorpe Wood. Take the path descending left through the woods, exit the woods and keep right still descending into the valley bottom. Cross the pasture towards the woods ahead, join a track leading up through the woods, where this turns left keep uphill on a fainter path to reach a gate at the

edge of the woods. Follow a narrow path into High Stittenham, cross a stile beside the pond and keep diagonally left across the field, cross the hedge and keep on descending to Cross Hill Farm. Pass to the right of this and then cross the field beyond

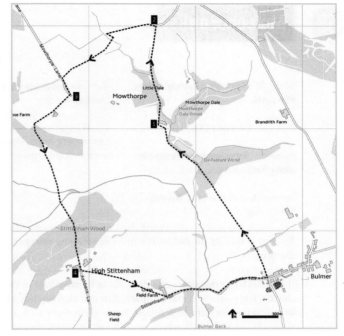

to reach the road. Turn left alongside and follow it climbing back to Bulmer village.

Points of interest

Bulmer village – The seat of the ancient wapentake of the same name. The name comes from 'bull mere', a lake frequented by a bull. It is mentioned in the Domesday Book, recorded in 1066 as belonging to a Northmann and Ligulf. By the 1900s, the lordship of the manor had passed to the Earls of Carlisle, who lived at Castle Howard. The monument to George William Frederick Howard can be found outside the village, on top of Bulmer Hill.

START At SE535771, Coxwold village, YO61 4DA

DISTANCE 5¼ miles (8.5 km)

SUMMARY A moderate walk mainly along field paths

PARKING Car park on the Byland Abbey road

MAPS Explorer 300; OS Sheets Landranger 100

WHERE TO EAT AND DRINK The Fauconberg Arms, Coxwold www.fauconbergarms.com

A lovely walk linking two of the AONBs villages, with great views from the ridge.

1 From the crossroads, go uphill though the village towards the church. Keep on as far the footpath sign just past Shandy Hall. Go left here, leaving the road, and follow the field edge to join a track. Go right along this over the hill, which provides great views over to Beacon Banks to the south. Keep along the field edge to a track leading to Coxwold Park House. Cross this and follow the hedge to join the track beyond the buildings. Go right along it and follow to Angram Hall. Pass through the yard to cross Twattleton Beck.

2 Leave the lane by going left across the field to join a road. Go left along this as far as the bridge over Elphin Beck. Just before this, go right through a gate, and cross the pasture towards Baxby Mill. Pass to the left of the old buildings. A rough track leads to Ings Lane. Go left to a junction where you go left again to Baxby Manor. Go right in front of this and follow the lane down to the road.

3 Go left along the road into Husthwaite village. Keep along the road through the charming village to a small triangle green. Keep right along The Nooking, for a few hundred metres to a narrow track between the house. Leave the road here and follow the track up through fields to emerge onto another road. Go left, then after a short distance go right along a lane. Follow this past houses, then climb up to the trig point on

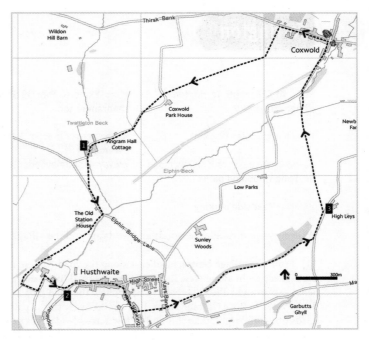

Beacon Banks, which provides a grand viewpoint over the surrounding countryside and beyond. Keep on along the escarpment to reach a lane, go left along this to High Leys Farm.

④ Leave the lane by going left over a stile just before the buildings. Descend, steeply at first, through the fields back towards Coxwold. At the bottom, cross Mill Beck via a footbridge, then left over the field to join the road. Go right along this back into the village.

Points of interest

Coxwold village – Mentioned in the Domesday Book by the name of Cucvalt, as part of the Yalestre hundred. At the time of the Norman invasion, the lord of the manor was Kofse, but passed to Hugh, son of. The name is derived from the Saxon word Cuc (cry) and valt (wood).

64 Terrington

Sᴛᴀʀᴛ At SE670706, Terrington village, YO60 6PP	Mᴀᴘs Explorer 300; OS Sheets Landranger 100
Dɪsᴛᴀɴᴄᴇ 5¼ miles (8.5 km)	Wʜᴇʀᴇ ᴛᴏ ᴇᴀᴛ ᴀɴᴅ ᴅʀɪɴᴋ Yorkshire Lavender
Sᴜᴍᴍᴀʀʏ An easy walk mainly along field and woodland paths	www.yorkshirelavender.com
Pᴀʀᴋɪɴɢ Roadside parking	

A lovely walk through the woods and fields around the village.

① From the village centre, head east along the road. Where it forks, keep right along New Road. Where the road turns sharp left, keep straight ahead on New Road. Follow the road past Low Water to Rose Cottage Farm. Just after passing this, a path leads off on the right, take this and follow across field edges to a footbridge over Wath Beck. Cross this and go left following the stream to a fence. Cross and go diagonally right across the field to a track.

② Go right along the track and in a short distance, go right again at the junction. Follow to a fork at the top of a hill. Keep left to shortly enter woods. Follow the path through the woods for about a mile to reach a road.

③ Go right along the road as far as the edge of the woods on the left. Go through the gate on your left into the field and go along the edge of the woods. Pass a couple of fences close together, at the next one, go right along it to a ditch. Go left alongside this to the corner of a wood, go right in front of this and cross fields to join Broats Lane. Continue along this to where it joins the road, at a T-junction. Keep straight ahead and follow the road back to Terrington village.

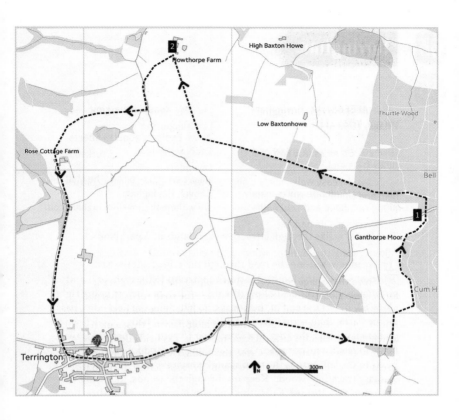

Points of interest

Yorkshire Lavender – Just outside Terrington village is the lavender farm/tourist attraction with tearooms, gift shops and attractions.

65

66

Hovingham

START At SE667755, Hovingham
village, YO62 4LF

DISTANCE 5½ miles (8.9 km) or 9
miles (14.5 km)

SUMMARY Moderate walks mainly
along woodland and field paths

PARKING Roadside parking

MAPS Explorer 300; OS Sheets
Landranger 100

WHERE TO EAT AND DRINK The Malt
Shovel, Hovingham
www.themaltshovelhovingham.com

Two lovely walks through attractive woodlands and parklands.

[1] Head north along the road through the village. At the Spa
Tearooms, cross the footbridge over the stream to the right of it and
go left along Brookside. Follow this a short distance before going right
along a lane. At the end of the houses, go left along the field edge, pass
Home Farm, then across the field following an old hedge. Go left when
you are level with the edge of a wood over to your left, then cross two
fields to reach a minor road. Go right along this and follow it until it
bears to the left. Just as the road straightens, leave it by going left along
a grassy track into woods. Keep on through the woods, following the
stream to a footbridge. Cross this and continue in the same direction to
join the track leading to Hovingham Lodge. Go left along this, keep left
onto the road passing the lodge and keep ahead to a sharp right turn. Go
left here and follow a track over fields to a road. Go right along it to the
entrance to Moor House Farm.

[2] Go left along the track and follow it over fields to Airyholme Farm.
Pass to the left of this to join a track in the woods.

[3] Go left along this and follow it through the woods. Cross a wet
section, then climb up through South Wood, ignoring any side tracks to
exit the woods at the top of the hill. Keep on along the track along field
edges to reach the road just outside the village. Go right back to the start.

[4] For the longer walk, at Moor House Farm, keep on along the road to
where it turns sharp right. Leave it and go left along a bridleway, heading

downhill to a corner of a wood. Go right onto a track along the side of a field and follow it, passing Rose Cottage Farm, and then onto New Road, which is followed into Terrington village. At the road junction, go left along New Back Lane, and follow it to the church.

⑤ Go left along a grassy track between houses, then right behind the houses down across fields, keeping left at the field corner. Keep ahead along the hedge line to climb up onto Huskit Hill, where a track is joined. Go left along this, follow it past Howthorpe Farm. At the edge of the woods, go left towards Airyholme Farm.

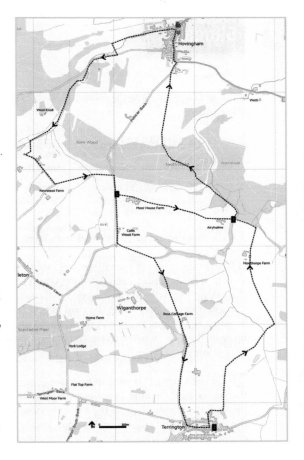

Points of interest

Hovingham Hall – Home to the Worsley family and the childhood home of the Duchess of Kent, with great views over Ryedale.

67 Slingsby

Start At SE698748, Slingsby village, YO62 4AQ

Distance 5½ miles (8.9 km)

Summary An easy walk mainly along field and woodland paths

Parking Roadside parking

Maps Explorer 300; OS Sheets Landranger 100

Where to eat and drink The Grapes Inn, Slingsby
www.thegrapesinn-slingsby.co.uk

A walk along an ancient earthwork with lovely views.

1 From the centre of the village, head south along Railway Street. At the junction, keep left along Green Dyke Lane, and then along The Balk. Keep along this to the crossroads, go straight over and keep along the road to bear left. Leave the road by going right along the grassy track, Back Lane, which climbs up onto Slingsby Heights. At the top of the climb, the Centenary Way is joined.

2 Go right along this path, at first along the edge of woodland, then entering them after crossing a couple of fields. Keep along through the woods, to cross the end of Fryton Lane. Continue in the same direction still through woods, eventually to arrive at a crossroads on the track at the corner of the wood.

3 Go right along the edge of the woods. On reaching the corner, keep ahead in the same direction, descending alongside quarry workings. On reaching the road, go right for a short distance, then left onto a bridleway, which dog legs to cross a stream and heads roughly north along the field edge to a track at the end of the field.

4 Go right along this and follow it. Cross Fryton Lane again and pass to the left of the house. Just after passing a small pond surrounded by trees, you will pass houses on your right. Turn

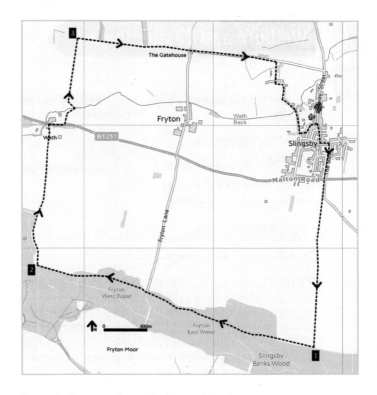

right onto a footpath that runs alongside them to join the access track. Keep left and follow this back into Slingsby village. On reaching the church, go left and follow Church Lane back to the centre of the village.

Points of interest

Slingsby – Part of the Hovingham Manor, this passed to the Mowbray family until John de Mowbray was beheaded in 1322 for rising against the Crown. The Mowbrays built a castle in the village, which fell into disrepair by 1345, around the same time the Hastings built another. The Cavendishes removed this and rebuilt where its remains can still be seen today, off the High Street.

68

69

Welburn and Castle Howard

START At SE721679, Welburn village, YO60 7DZ

DISTANCE 5½ miles (8.9 km) or 10 miles (16.9 km)

SUMMARY Moderate walks mainly along woodland and field paths

PARKING Roadside parking

MAPS Explorer 300; OS Sheets Landranger 100

WHERE TO EAT AND DRINK The Crown and Cushion www.thecrownandcushionwelburn.com

Two interesting walks through attractive woodlands and parklands.

[1] Head west along the road, through the village. At the end of the houses go right along a track. Pass through the farm yard, keep on. At the facing hedge, go right, then left at the corner. Go left through the hedge as the hedge curves away. Follow field edges to Moor House, climb alongside the edge of a wood to reach a road. Go left along this and follow it to the junction with The Stray, beside an imposing gateway.

[2] Go right along The Stray and follow it for about 1½ miles to the crossroads, there are good views on the right across the Great Lake and Castle Howard. At the crossroads, go right into Coneysthorpe. Keep on through the village until a white gate in the wall on the right is reached. Go through this, and then diagonally left to a track. Go right to a T-junction.

[3] Go left and then go right into trees, keeping left, and following the track through woods into parkland. Go right along the wall, crossing grass to New River Bridge. Cross this and keep ahead to reach crossroads. Go straight over to the edge of woodlands.

[4] Go downhill diagonally through the woods, cross Moorhouse Beck at the bottom, and then follow the track back to Welburn.

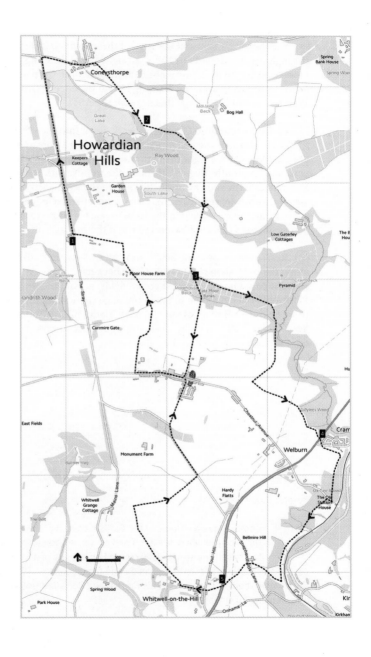

(5) For the longer route, at the edge of the woodlands, keep left through the woods; at Four Faces, straight ahead, heading down to cross Moorhouse Beck. Keep ahead at the junction, the path climbs before contouring around Chanting Hill to the edge of Gillylees Wood. Go right and follow this to reach the A64.

(6) Cross the road into Crambeck, walk down into the village, then right through the hedge. Pass to the right of a house to reach Ox Carr Woods. Go right through the woods and follow the path heading south. Keep on through the woods, with the River Derwent and the railway line below you to the left, shortly after where the railway runs close to the river on a bend. Go diagonally right uphill through a gap in the trees to reach a lane. Go straight across the road and field beyond to reach the A64 again.

(7) Re-cross this, over the field into Whitwell-on-the-Hill. Go left along the road, then right along a lane between houses. At the end go right past a house, then left across fields, behind the woods of Whitwell Hotel. Keep on to join a track, go right along this, over three fields to Whitwell Road. Turn left along this and follow it, heading for Welburn village, keeping right where it forks on the edge of the woods back to the village.

Points of interest

Castle Howard – Home of the Carlisle branch of the Howard family for over 300 years. It's not a real castle, but the term also applies to English country houses created on the site of a former military castle. The castle is known to television and film audiences as the fictional *Brideshead*, both in Evelyn Waugh's *Brideshead Revisited* (1981) and the two hour remake for cinema (2008).

The City of Troy

START At SE649726, Scackleton village, YO62 4NB

DISTANCE 6 miles (9.7 km)

SUMMARY An easy walk mainly along field paths

PARKING Roadside parking

MAPS Explorer 300; OS Sheets Landranger 100

WHERE TO EAT AND DRINK None

A varied walk with fine views over the Howardian Hills.

[1] Leave the village by heading north-west along Scackleton Lane. Just before the fork, go left along Grange Lane, which is followed to Scackleton Grange. At the farm, go right to pass through the yard, exit through a gate and follow the left hand fence. Where this turns sharp left, follow it to descend to cross a stream. The path contours around the hillside, then drops again to cross another stream. Keep straight ahead, climbing to Swathgill Spring.

[2] Go left along the fence on a path that curves around Leys Hill then, descending to Potter Hill Farm. Pass between the buildings onto the access road. Where this bears to the left, keep right along a track, which climbs gently to the edge of Mug Dale Wood. Join another track here, go left along it through the woods. Descend to a crossroads of track, keep alongside the stream, the track then climbs. Keep following to a junction at the edge of woods. Go right and continue to the road.

[3] Go left along Bonnygate Lane, passing the City of Troy maze on the left. Keep on to a footpath sign on the right. Leave the road here and go right across the field into the woods. Climb through these to join a road. Go right along this, keep right at the junction with Low Lane. At the third group of houses, go left along a track, just before the telephone box. Stay on this over fields to join Low Lane, beside a house. Go right along the road, passing the church to a T-junction. Turn left to a footpath sign.

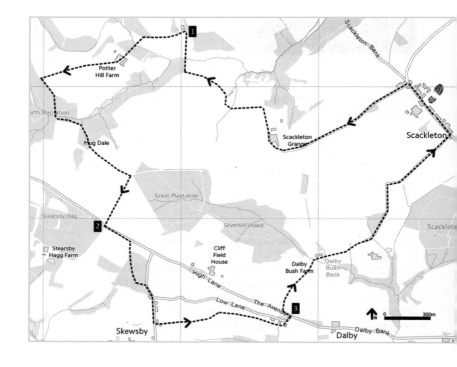

④ Go right along a track, descending to Dalby Bush Farm. Pass to the right of this. A track crosses fields to join another track near to Scackleton Low Moor. Keep left along this and follow this over fields back towards the village. Go left at the junction back to the start.

Points of interest

🔍 The City of Troy – The smallest turf maze in Europe; references to the ancient City of Troy are common in maze names. Like other ancient turf mazes, this maze was almost certainly used for religious and fertility rituals.

Coneysthorpe Bank

START **At SE735735, Barton-le-Street village, YO17 6PH**

DISTANCE **6 miles (9.7 km)**

SUMMARY **A moderate walk mainly along field and woodland paths**

PARKING **Roadside parking**

MAPS **Explorer 300; OS Sheets Landranger 100**

WHERE TO EAT AND DRINK **The Cresswell Arms, Appleton-le-Street www.cresswellarms.co.uk**

A fine walk along an ancient earthwork bank with grand views.

1 Leave the village green by heading east along Butterwick Road. At the T-junction, go right along Back Lane, passing Glebe Farm. Where the road turns right, keep left onto a track, which is followed across fields to eventually emerge onto the B1257. Go left along the road into Appleton-le-Street village, towards the Cresswell Arms.

2 Go right beside the pub, along Willow Bank Lane. Keep along this as it climbs through fields to reach Amotherby Lane. Go right along this to the T-junction.

3 Go right along the road for a short distance, then go left, beside a small triangular section of grass. Follow this track downhill through woods. Go right into the woods, passing a farm on your left. The track runs along the edge of the woods, before climbing to reach a road. Go straight across this towards Park House, pass to the left of this and follow the edge of the woods, over fields at first, then into the woods, to a junction with Appleton Lane.

4 Keep ahead and stay on the track through the woods for about ½ mile, exit them and keep left along the edge of the woods. Pass the trig point, shortly after this go right onto Kirk Road and descend towards the village. On reaching the B1257, go right and then left back into the village.

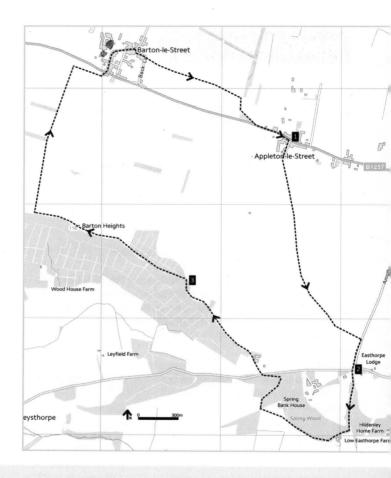

Points of interest

🔍 Coneysthorpe Bank – This is an ancient earthwork extending over 2 km through Coneysthorpe Banks Woods, it is a scheduled monument. This section of dyke is well preserved as an earthwork and significant archaeological remains will be retained within the bank and ditch. The dyke is part of a wider system of boundaries, enclosures and ritual sites.

Sheriff Hutton

START At SE652663, Sheriff Hutton village, YO60 6QZ

DISTANCE 6½ miles (10.5 km)

SUMMARY A moderate walk mainly along field paths and tracks

PARKING Roadside parking

MAPS Explorer 300; OS Sheets Landranger 100

WHERE TO EAT AND DRINK The Highway Man, Sheriff Hutton www.thehighwayman.uk.com

A pleasant walk from a colourful historic village.

1 From the village centre head south along Finkle Street, past The Highway Man pub. Where the road turns to the right, leave the road by going left along a path beside a bungalow, passing behind the village hall. Keep on in the same direction, over fields to West Lilling village.

2 Go left along the road for a short distance, then right onto New Lane. Follow this, downhill, to a T-junction. Go right along the road and keep on to another T-junction.

3 Go left and follow the road. Just after crossing over the River Foss, go right through the hedge and follow the path along the stream to Foss House. Go right along a track, passing in front of the house. At the next junction, go left onto another track over fields to Cornsborough Farm.

4 After passing the farm, go right into a field, following a fence on the right. At the corner, keep on in the same direction, aiming for a grassy track. At the end of the field go right, and climb alongside the field edge towards Cornborough Manor. At the junction of tracks, go right, then at the T-junction go left, to pass in front of an electricity sub-station. Keep on in the same direction over fields to Mill Hill Farm. Pass to the right of it to a junction of paths.

⑤ Go straight ahead over the field in front. At the far side, bear diagonally right to the corner of the next field. Another path is joined. Go left through the gate and keep to the left edge of the field, hedges on both sides soon appear. Keep on the Green Lane back into the village centre.

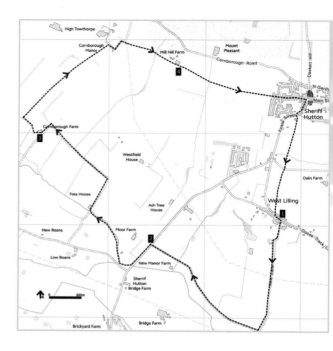

Points of interest

🔍 **Sheriff Hutton Castle** – Quadrangular in form, with four corner towers connected by ranges of buildings that enclose an inner courtyard. The northern and western sides are straight, while the south and east contain outward pointing angles at their centres. The entrance is in the east wall, which a gatehouse protects. The ranges of buildings and curtain walls between have mostly gone and only sections of the towers remain at their original height. A middle and outer ward originally existed, now covered by the adjacent farm. A Grade II listed building, the castle is recognized as a structure of international importance.

Nunnington

START At SE669782, top of Caukleys Bank, YO62 4LH

DISTANCE 6½ miles (10.5 km)

SUMMARY An easy walk mainly along field and riverside paths

PARKING Roadside parking

MAPS Explorer 300; OS Sheets Landranger 100

WHERE TO EAT AND DRINK The Royal Oak, Nunnington www.nunningtonroyaloak.co.uk

A pleasant walk with good views over the surrounding countryside.

① From the top of the road, head west along the ridge on the bridleway. Keep on this to enter woods, descending to join another bridleway. Go right along to the road, go right along this, passing the impressive Stonegrave Minster on the left to reach a footpath sign on the right.

② Go through the gate and follow the track steeply uphill. At the top, the track curves around the field then turns sharp right to cross two fields to a road. Go left for a short distance, leave the road going right along a path heading towards woods. Before reaching the woods, go left across a field to join High Moor Lane. Go right along this to the edge of more woods. Leave the lane here and go right through the woods to reach the banks of the River Rye. Turn right and follow the river to the road in Nunnington village.

③ Go left and follow Church Street through the pretty village, keeping left at the church onto Low Street. Keep on this to the T-junction, go right here for a short distance, then left over a stile in a lane. Pass alongside woodlands then fields to Mill Farm, passing to the left of this along the river bank. Follow the river again to Ness Bridge where a road is joined. Go right along this and follow it to a T-junction.

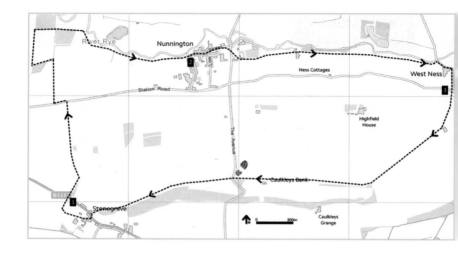

④ Go to the left and then leave the road by going right onto Caulkley's Lane, which climbs gently up Caulkleys Bank. At the fork in the track, keep right, still climbing towards the top of the hill and trig point, which provides a grand viewpoint. From here it's a short walk along the ridge back to the road.

Points of interest

Nunnington Hall – A National Trust property open to the public. It has an interesting collection of doll's houses.

Ampleforth

START At SE578786, Ampleforth
village, YO62 4DA

DISTANCE 6¾ miles (10.9 km)

SUMMARY A moderate walk mainly
along field and woodland paths

PARKING Roadside parking

MAPS Explorer 300; OS Sheets
Landranger 100

WHERE TO EAT AND DRINK The White
Swan
www.thewhiteswan-ampleforth.
co.uk

A walk through the undulating Howardian Hills.

1 Leave the road through Ampleforth by going south-east along a track between houses, and follow it alongside a stream over fields to Mill Farm and another road. Go left along the road, until it makes a sharp left turn. Leave it here and go right onto a track beside a house. Follow the track alongside field edges, to enter woods. Keep on to cross a disused railway and then along the field edge to reach a road. Cross this and go diagonally left towards the corner of a lake and a track. Go right along this. Ignore tracks going off on the left to reach to smaller lakes.

2 Go right on a track between them, to a track junction, go left and then almost immediately right. Follow this past a house, then keep on along it, ignoring all the side paths to reach North Moor Lane. Go right and follow the road to where it makes a sharp right turn. Leave it and go left through the hedge, then diagonally left across the field. Almost double back on yourself by going right along the edge of woods. Keep on in the same direction over fields to reach Low Lions Lodge. Pass between the barns onto a track, keep left at the junction. Keep on over fields at a T-junction.

3 Go right to pass Old Pilfit. Keep on, the track bears to the right around woods. Go left through a gate and over a field. At the end of the hedge/fence, go left across the field and along the edge of woods to a pond. Go diagonally right away from this, passing the corner of

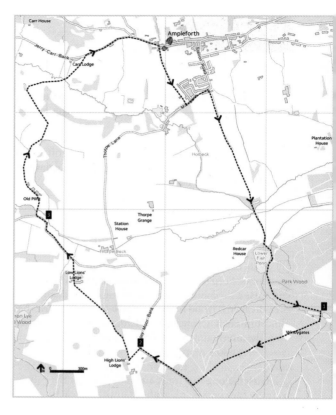

woods. Keep on uphill in the same direction through rough pastures to reach the road. Go right along this and walk back into Ampleforth.

Points of interest

Ampleforth Abbey – A monastery of Benedictine Monks, part of the English Benedictine Congregation and a mile to the east of Ampleforth village. Sigebert Buckley (1520-1610), the last surviving monk from Westminster, claimed descent from the pre-Reformation community at Westminster Abbey.

Sheriff Hutton

START At SE652663, Sheriff Hutton village, YO60 6QZ

DISTANCE 7 miles (11.2 km)

SUMMARY A moderate walk mainly along field paths and tracks

PARKING Roadside parking

MAPS Explorer 300; OS Sheets Landranger 100

WHERE TO EAT AND DRINK The Highway Man, Sheriff Hutton
www.thehighwayman.uk.com

A pleasant walk on the edge of the Howardian Hills.

1 Walk east along Main Street, through the village. Where the road forks, keep left along East End and follow it to where the houses end. Pass a shed and then go left along the field edge and ahead over the field beyond to the road. Go right along the road, and then almost immediately left into Carr Lane. At the corner of a hedge, leave the lane and go right along the hedge to reach a track junction, just after passing a small pond on your right.

2 Go left along this track and follow it over the gallops, used for training race horses. Keep ahead until you reach a footbridge over Ings Beck. Cross this and go left along the beck to the end of the field. Here, turn right towards Primrose Farm. Pass through the yard onto a track, follow this uphill through the woods. At the top, ignore the track going left, and keep ahead across the field to join Mowthorpe Lane.

3 Go right along this to the junction leading to Mowthorpe Hill Farm. Go right along the track towards the buildings, passing to the right of them to the edge of Mowthorpe Wood. Take the path descending left through the woods, exit the woods and keep right, still descending into the valley bottom. Cross the pasture towards the woods ahead. Join a track leading up through the woods, where this turns left keep uphill on a fainter path to reach a gate at the edge of the woods. Follow a narrow path into High Stittenham.

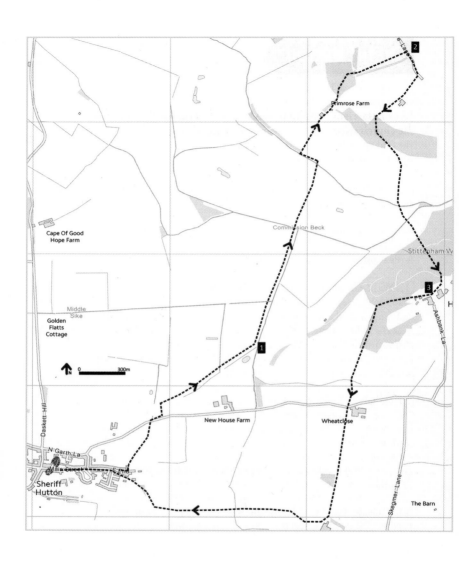

Cape Of Good
Hope Farm

Commission Beck

Primrose Farm

Stittenham W

Ashbank La

Middle
Sike

Golden
Flatts
Cottage

0   300m
N

Daskett Hill

N Garth La

Main Street   S End

Sheriff
Hutton

New House Farm

Wheatclose

Skegmer Lane

The Barn

1

2

3

(3) Go right past the houses, and follow the road past Hall Farm into the woods. Keep left where this forks, going downhill to exit the woods. Cross the fields heading towards Wheatclose, crossing a beck before reaching a road. Go straight over and pass to the left of the farm buildings, then over fields to Sheepclose. Go through the gate on the right, across a paddock, into fields beyond, aiming for the church spire. Cross a stream into a hedged lane; follow this. At the end go right to enter the churchyard. Go left through this back into the village.

Points of interest

Sheriff Hutton Castle – Quadrangular in form, with four corner towers connected by ranges of buildings that enclose an inner courtyard. The northern and western sides are straight, while the south and east contain outward pointing angles at their centres. The entrance is in the east wall, which a gatehouse protects. The ranges of buildings and curtain walls between have mostly gone and only sections of the towers remain at their original height. A middle and outer ward originally existed, now covered by the adjacent farm. A Grade II listed building, the castle is recognized as a structure of international importance.

76 Kilburn

START At SE512796, Kilburn village, YO61 4AH

DISTANCE 8 miles (12.9 km)

SUMMARY A moderate walk mainly along woodland and field paths

PARKING Roadside parking

MAPS Explorer OL26; OS Sheets Landranger 100

WHERE TO EAT AND DRINK The Forresters Arms, Kilburn www.forrestersarms.com

An undulating walk linking Kilburn village with Byland Abbey.

① Leave the village by going through the churchyard, then along the uphill path, bearing right at the top into High Kilburn. Cross the village green to the road, go right along this and follow it to a footpath sign on the left, opposite a junction.

② Keep left along the road, until just before it makes a sharp left turn. Leave it and go right along a grassy path. Follow this through trees, where these spot. Keep ahead a short distance to the facing trees, go right along these, to a gap. Go left to shortly cross a stream. Keep ahead over fields to a farm, then go right in front of the buildings to join the road. Go left along this, past the houses to the junction with Sand Lane.

③ Go right along Sand Lane, bear right past the houses, to enter woods. At the junction go right, then keep left at the next. Follow the track through the woods for about a mile. At the T-junction go right, and then right again at the next junction. The track exits the woods. Keep ahead to Cam House. Go right to pass the house and farm beyond, keeping to the right hand edge of the fields. At the junction of three fences, go right and follow the fence over fields to more woods. Enter the woods onto a track, follow this and go left at the first junction. At the next junction, go left downhill, then right at the following junction. Keep along the track to cross a stream, then go right along another track to reach a read.

④ Go along this a short distance, before going right into a field. Follow

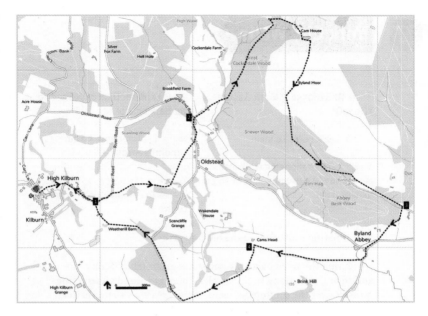

the edge of woods around to a farm. Pass to the left of this onto its access track. Go left along this to the road. Go right along the road, passing Byland Abbey. Keep on past the pub to a gap in the hedge. Go right over the stile and follow the path over fields, towards Cam Heads. Keep to the left of the farm, and at the end of the field, level with it.

5 Go left along the hedge, then follow the edge of the woods to a road. Go right along this and follow it to where it turns sharp right. Leave the road and keep ahead through trees. Where these end, go left over fields to Weatherill Barn. Go right onto a track and follow to the road.

6 Go left and retrace outward route back to the village.

Points of interest

Byland Abbey – Founded in 1135 by monks who moved there from Old Byland Abbey as it was too close to Rievaulx Abbey.

START At SE605522, Monk Bar Gate, YO1 7LQ

DISTANCE 2¾ miles (4.5 km)

SUMMARY A challenging walk mainly along the old city walls, lots of steps to negotiate

PARKING Numerous pay and display car parks in the city centre

MAPS Explorer 290; OS Sheets Landranger 105

WHERE TO EAT AND DRINK Various places to eat and drink in the city centre

A fascinating walk around the old city walls.

1 Climb the steep narrow stone stairs to the left of Monk Bar, and then go left along the city walls. There are grand views of the minster over the rooftops/gardens of the Treasurer's House. Keep on along the walls to reach Bootham Bar.

2 Descend the stairs back down to street level. Go right through the stone gateway, then left onto St Leonards Place. Cross over the road and go right a short distance, then left towards the Kings Manor and the Yorkshire Museum. Walk through the gardens in front of these, to reach the banks of the river. Go left to steps back up to road level, then right along Station Road, over the bridge.

3 At the far side of the bridge, go right, climbing back up onto the city walls. There are good views back towards York Minster from here. Pass the railway station down to your right and keep on past Micklegate Bar, then in front of houses on your left, to reach Baile Hill.

4 Leave the city wall again, by descending steps onto Skeldergate. Go left to cross over the river again. Keep right along Tower Street in front of the castle, to cross the River Foss. In front of you is Postern Tower. Rejoin the city wall trail here. Go right along the wall, and keep on passing Walmgate Bar to Red Tower, where the city walls end. Descend to street level and go left towards Foss

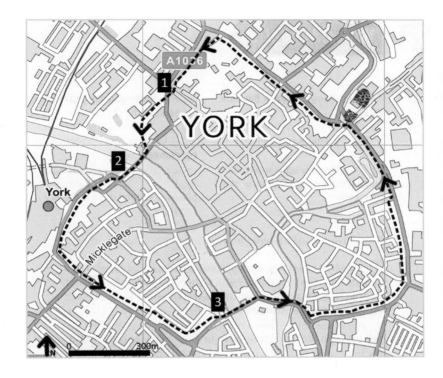

Islands Road, first past houses but soon to join the banks of the River Foss. There were never any walls built along this section as the city was protected by the river/marshes. Keep on to traffic lights, go left over the river, then cross over to the city wall on the other side of the road. Go left along the walls until you reach Monk Bar. There's one final section of stairs back down to the starting point.

Points of interest

York has many points of interest in the city centre far too numerous to list here.

START At SE731509, Wilberfoss village, YO41 5NN

DISTANCE 3 miles (4.8 km)

SUMMARY An easy walk on field paths with some road walking

PARKING Roadside parking

MAPS Explorer 290; OS Sheets Landranger 105

WHERE TO EAT AND DRINK The Oddfellow Arms www.oddfellowsarmswilberfoss. co.uk

An interesting walk around the environs of the village.

[1] From the village green, cross over the footbridge onto Beckside. Go left along this, pass a second footbridge, then shortly after go right along a narrow path between houses. Keep along the path, cross over Woldview Road, and then over Field Head. At the end of the houses, join a track leading to some allotments, go right along it. Where this turns right towards them, keep straight ahead between fields. Pass under power lines and keep alongside a ditch over fields to reach Carberry Hall Farm. Go right through the farm yard, then right onto a track. Go left along the field edge/ hedge. Where this turns sharp left, go diagonally right across the field, through a gap in the hedge. Keep across the field to a gate, go through this, then go left alongside the hedge over three fields to join a road opposite Fat Rabbit Farm.

[2] Go left along Ling Lane, which follows back to Wilberfoss village. Pass the 30mph speed limit signs and the first group of houses. Keep along the road until just after crossing over a stream. Go left through small gates into a field then go right to join the banks of Foss Beck. As the houses are reached, go along a narrow path between them to emerge onto Middlecroft and go right onto Middle Street. At the junction with Main Street, go left and follow it back to the village green.

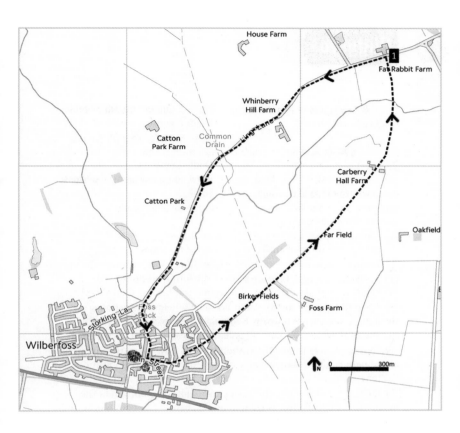

Points of interest

Wilberfoss – Elias de Cotton founded the priory of Benedictine nuns at Wilberfoss during the reign of Henry II. At the time, the Suppression of the Monasteries by Henry VIII had a yearly value of £26. 10s. 8d. The priory lay to the north of St John's Church but there are no remains left.

Huggate

Sᴛᴀʀᴛ At SE881552, Huggate village, YO42 1YH

Dɪsᴛᴀɴᴄᴇ 4 miles (6.5 km) or 9 miles (14.4 km)

Sᴜᴍᴍᴀʀʏ Moderate walks mainly along woodland and field paths

Pᴀʀᴋɪɴɢ Limited roadside parking

Mᴀᴘs Explorer 294; OS Sheets Landranger 106

Wʜᴇʀᴇ ᴛᴏ ᴇᴀᴛ ᴀɴᴅ ᴅʀɪɴᴋ The Wolds Inn www.woldsinn.co.uk

Two interesting walks through typical Wolds countryside.

1 From the crossroads, go north along Stocks Hill, through the village. When the houses end, keep on to a track leading off on the left.

2 Keep right along the road, climbing over fields, then through an avenue of cherry trees towards Northfield House. At a signpost at a fence corner, leave the road and go left along a grassy track to a gate overlooking Horse Dale. Go through it and follow the path sloping down to the right to some pens.

3 Go through the gates and then go left along the bottom of the steep sided Horse Dale. Follow this for about 1½ miles. The path climbs up to a gate, go through this, then go left alongside the hedge along a track. At the field end, go right across to join a road. Go left along this to Glebe Farm, go right in front of the farm along a track. Follow this back to Huggate village and go right uphill back to the start.

4 For the longer walk, go through the gate and keep straight ahead, climbing through Holme Dale. At the top where it forks, keep left, climbing to reach a gate. Join a track here which is followed over fields to Wold House Farm. Keep right between buildings as you enter the yard, then go diagonally left across the next yard onto a track. Go right along this to York Lane.

5 Go right along the road to a T-junction. Leave the road and go left down into trees along a track. Leave the track by keeping right onto a

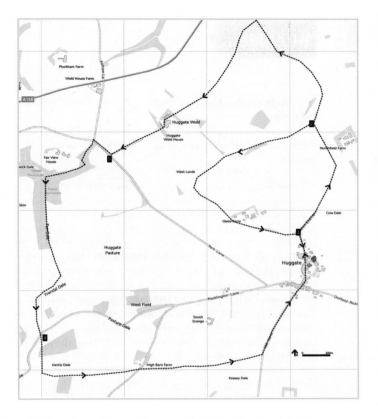

path. Follow this first through trees, then over fields to join a track in the bottom of Greenwick Dale. Go left along this and follow it through Tun Dale, keeping right into Frendale to reach a road.

⑥ Go left along the road a short distance, then right through a gate to climb steeply up the side of Pasture Dale. At a gate above Nettle Dale, don't descend, keep left along the fence line and follow this around the top of Nettle Dale to a stile. Cross this and go left along a track, follow this over fields to a lane opposite Cobdale Cottage. Go across the road and through a gate to the left of the cottage onto another wide track, Hawold Bridie Road. Keep along this over fields as it slowly descends towards Keasey Dale, to join Mill Lane. Go left along this and follow it back into Huggate village.

81 Kirkham

START At SE734658, Kirkham Priory, YO60 7JS

DISTANCE 5 miles (8 km)

SUMMARY A moderate walk on field and riverside paths

PARKING Roadside parking

MAPS Explorer 300; OS Sheets Landranger 100

WHERE TO EAT AND DRINK The Stonetrough Inn

A pleasant walk along the banks of the River Derwent.

(1) From the parking area, go left over Kirkham Bridge. Continue along the road, just after the level crossing the road begins to climb and curves to the right. After a short distance, go left along a track leading through woodland. This climbs steeply through the trees to join a road. Go left along this and walk into Crambe village. At the T-junction, go right towards the church. Pass this and keep on, keep right at the bend and continue between the houses to a footpath sign. Go left here, cross a field, and then a stream via a footbridge. Climb steeply up the opposite bank to join a track, go left along it, still climbing. Keep on the track to a facing fence, just before it starts to descend.

(2) Go left along the fence/hedge across Crambe Bank to join a track descending across the field. Go right and follow this downhill, crossing the railway line again to reach Rider Lane Farm. Pass to the right of this to join the access track which is followed to the road. Go right along the road and follow it for about ½ mile to a footpath sign on the left.

(3) Leave the road and go left along the hedge, crossing a field to reach the banks of the River Derwent. Turn left and follow the pleasant riverside path over several fields back to Kirkham Bridge. Go right over the bridge to the parking area.

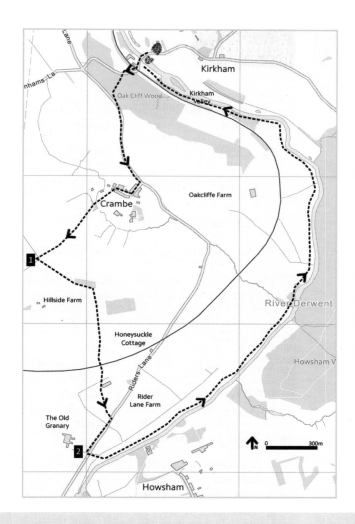

Points of interest

🔍 Kirkham Priory – A well maintained ruin. Founded in 1130 by Augustinian monks and is open to the public.

START **At SE797550, Bishop Wilton village, YO42 1RX**

DISTANCE **6 miles (9.7 km)**

SUMMARY **A moderate walk mainly on field paths**

PARKING **Roadside parking**

MAPS **Explorer 300; OS Sheets Landranger 100**

WHERE TO EAT AND DRINK **The Fleece Inn www.thefleeceinn.info**

An interesting walk through fields on the edge of the Wolds.

1 From the village centre, head north along Garrowby Road, then turn left into Vicarage Lane, just before the crossroads. Keep ahead along this to reach Thorny Lane, go right here and follow it to a T-junction. Turn left onto Bray Gate and follow this for about a mile to where it turns sharp right.

2 Keep left onto Ings Lane and follow this over fields. Where the surface lane turns left, keep straight ahead onto a grassy track. Follow this, and where the hedge on the left turns away to the left, keep straight ahead. Cross a stream and a field to reach Gowthorpe village. Do enter this, go left along a track over fields, which dog legs to reach Highfield Lane.

3 Go left along this and follow into Fangfoss village. Keep ahead through the village. Just after the pub, turn left and follow the lane leading to Jubilee Park. Pass to the right of the park, and keep along the track to a stream. Go left along it, and shortly after the track, turn right away from it towards High Belthorpe.

4 Turn right in front of the house onto its access track, Belthorpe Lane. Keep along this to the junction with Bolton Lane. Keep left to reach the junction with Thorny Lane. Go right into Bishop Wilton and follow the road through the village back to the start.

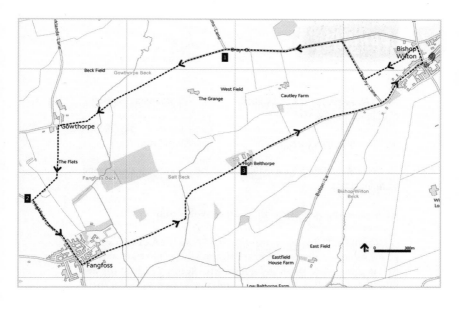

Points of interest

Bishop Wilton – A beautifully placed village just below the ridge of the Wolds. The church spire is very prominent and a pleasant stream runs through the village.

Bainton

START At SE9645268, a layby north
of Bainton village, YO25 9NR

DISTANCE 6¼ miles (10 km)

SUMMARY A moderate walk mainly
on fields paths

PARKING Roadside parking

MAPS Explorer 294; OS Sheets
Landranger 106

WHERE TO EAT AND DRINK None

An undulating walk through pleasant Wolds countryside.

1 From the layby, cross over the A641 onto the footpath and
go left along the main road into Bainton village. Go right at the
first junction onto West End, follow this, keeping right at the next
junction, and follow the road through the houses. Where it turns
sharp right, leave it and go left on a muddy track to a gate. Go
through this and directly ahead over the field, aiming for a group of
trees in the distance. Pass to the right of these to a track leading to
a house and cross straight over this onto a track alongside the field
edge. Continue along this over three fields, then turn right to reach
the corner of a road.

2 Go left along the road towards North Dalton, follow it through
the village, until just after the telephone box. Turn right at the
entrance to Centre House Farm, onto Hudson's Lane. Follow this past
the farm buildings, then climb over fields, before descending to the
edge of woods in Deep Dale.

3 Descend through the trees. At the bottom go right along a path.
Keep on through the valley bottom fields to reach the corner of Low
Wood. Turn right uphill and follow the edge of the wood. When this
stops, keep ahead over the field to the left of woods facing you. Turn
left along the edge of these and follow them to reach the B1248. Go
right along this to the crossroads, go straight over and follow the road
back to the layby.

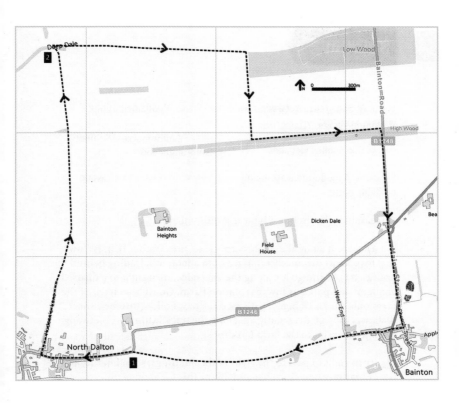

Points of interest

Bainton – The old church of St Andrew's is worth visiting. A socket
for an old stone cross is just inside the entrance.

START At SE933591, Wetwang village, YO25 9XJ

DISTANCE 6½ miles (10.5 km)

SUMMARY A moderate walk mainly on fields paths

PARKING Roadside parking

MAPS Explorer 294; OS Sheets Landranger 106

WHERE TO EAT AND DRINK None

A pleasant walk circling a typical Wolds village.

1 Head east along the A166, turning left into Station Hill. Follow this for a short distance to go right onto a footpath, leading behind the houses. At the end go left along the field edge, then right to a disused chalk pit, left past this towards Station Farm. Go right in front of the farm onto the track bed of a disused railway. Follow this for a short distance, then go diagonally left along the track leading to Wetwang Grange. Keep on to the farm buildings.

2 Turn right to pass to the right of the buildings, soon after re-join the old railway line. Turn left and follow this for about a mile, to where a track joins from the left. Go right here along the bridleway, follow it uphill over fields to the A166. Cross over and go slightly right onto another bridleway. Follow this over fields to join a track near to Little Grange.

3 Go right along this and keep on in the same direction to reach the B1248. Cross straight over this onto Green Lane. Follow this through the trees to the wide grassy track of Southfield Well Balk. Keep on in the same direction passing two more fields to a path junction.

4 Turn right here and follow the track gently downhill through Thorn Dale to the corner of a road. Go right along this for a short distance, then right through a gap in the hedge, just before a telegraph pole. Follow the path along the left side of the field back towards Wetwang. Exit the field onto Southfield Road, go right then left into Southfield Close. At the end of this, an alley leads back to the main road.

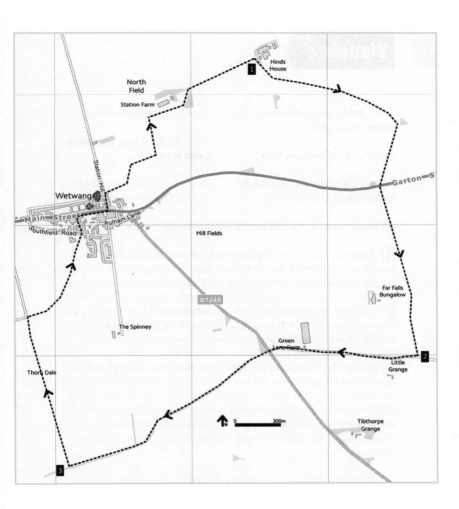

START At SE928645, Sledmere
village, YO25 3XG

DISTANCE 6½ miles (10.5 km)

SUMMARY A moderate walk mainly
on field and woodland paths

PARKING Roadside parking

MAPS Explorer 294; OS Sheets
Landranger 106

WHERE TO EAT AND DRINK The Triton Inn
www.thetritoninn.co.uk

A pleasant walk through undulating Wolds countryside.

[1] From the parking area go left along the B1251, past the
ornate memorial, and then left into Kirby Lane. Follow this for a
couple of miles until the edge of Kirby Plantation is reached.

[2] Go right here along the track towards Squirrel Hill Farm,
pass in front of this, and keep along the path on the edge of
woods. This eventually cuts through the woods at Fox Covert,
then goes right along the edge of the woods again. At the end
of the trees, keep ahead in the same direction over the field to a
junction of tracks.

[3] Go right here towards Thirkleby Wold. Join its access road
at the corner of trees, go left along this and follow it to join
Croome Road. Go right here and follow the road to the entrance
of Croome Farm.

[4] Keep along Croome Road for a short distance, then go left
into a field, via a stile. Walk parallel to the fence on your left to
reach a track. Go diagonally left to the corner of a wood. At the
end of the woods, go left along its edge and follow this around
the field boundary to reach the B1253. Go right along the road to
a T-junction with the B1252. Here, go right and follow the road
through the village back to the parking area.

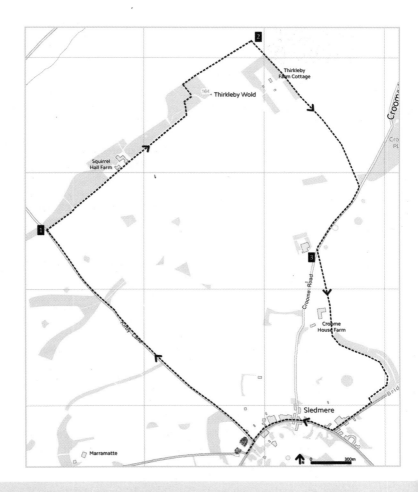

Points of interest

Sledmere House – A Georgian country house, set within a park designed by Capability Brown and now a Grade I listed building. The house was begun in 1751, extended during the 1790s, and rebuilt in 1911 after a fire. Once the home of Sir Mark Sykes, English traveller and diplomatic advisor, it now belongs to Sir Tatton Sykes, 8th Baronet.

86 Malton

START At SE786714, Malton Railway Station, YO17 7NR

DISTANCE 6½ miles (10.5 km)

SUMMARY An easy walk mainly on riverside paths with a section of quite road walking

PARKING Numerous pay and display car parks in Malton

MAPS Explorer 300; OS Sheets Landranger 100

WHERE TO EAT AND DRINK Various places to eat and drink in Malton

A fine walk along the banks of the River Derwent.

① From the railway station, go north along Railway Street towards the River Derwent, to go left onto Riverside View. Keep right at the play area to join the riverside path. Now follow the pleasant riverside path alongside the River Derwent as it meanders its way southwards. At one point the railway line squeezes you close to the riverbank, things widen out again and the walking is pleasant along the river. Not long after passing Cherry Islands, in the river, the path passes under the railway line and then soon afterwards, a suspension bridge of the river is reached. Don't cross this, keep half left through the trees to reach the road.

② Go left along the road, and then left again at the T-junction, onto Menethorpe Lane, keeping right at the next junction. Keep on along the road for about 1 mile, to where it turns sharp right. Leave here and go left onto a path between the trees, which is followed down into Grove Plantation. Keep right at the track junction at the bottom edge of the woods, and follow this to Welham Hall Farm. Here, go left onto a track, follow this past a lake and then over the golf course. At the club house, go right towards the car park entrance, then left along a narrow path. At the end of this a track is joined, go right along it, passing Star Cottage Stable to join Welham Road. Go left along this, and follow it through Norton to the level crossing. Go left over the railway line, then left again into Norton Road, which leads back to the station.

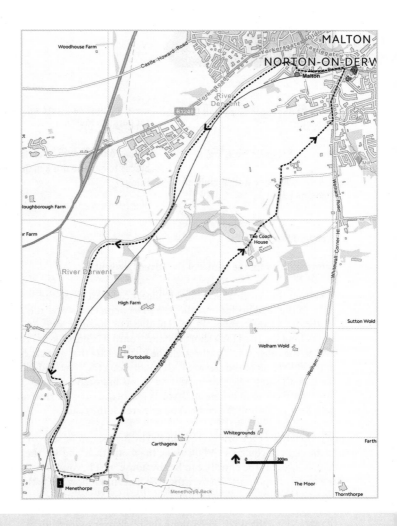

Points of interest

Malton – A very busy market town on the northern bank of the
River Derwent, close to its junction with the River Rye.

Stamford Bridge

START At SE711555, Stamford Bridge, YO41 1AF

DISTANCE 6¾ miles (10.8 km)

SUMMARY An easy walk mainly on riverside paths

PARKING Pay and display car parks in Stamford Bridge

MAPS Explorer 290; OS Sheets Landranger 105

WHERE TO EAT AND DRINK Various places to eat and drink in Stamford Bridge

A fine walk along the banks of the River Derwent.

[1] From the centre of Stamford Bridge, head west along the A166 to the road bridge over the River Derwent. Cross over the footbridge, to the right of the road bridge. On the other side, go right along the road for a short distance, until it is possible to cross over to the other side. Go through the kissing gate that gives access to the riverbank of the Derwent. Go right along the river and follow the path through riverside meadows. This is followed for about 3 miles until the road bridge at Kexby is reached. Leave the riverside path here and climb the embankment to reach the road.

[2] Go left over the bridge, the old Kexby Bridge can be seen over to the right as you cross. Walk along the footpath, alongside the A1079, as far as the entrance to Kexby house. Just beyond this there is a footpath signpost. Go over the stile here and follow the path alongside the hedge. Where this stops, keep on ahead in the same direction over two fields to some farm buildings. Pass to the left of them along the track, keep along the track over more fields to reach Town End Farm, where a road is joined. Go left along this and follow it through the village of Low Catton, to where it turns sharp right, outside The Old Rectory.

[3] Leave the road here, go through a gate to the right on the entrance to a house. Follow this through trees and then over fields

back towards Stamford Bridge. As you approach the outskirts of the town, keep to the left of the houses, onto the riverside. Go right along the river. Pass under a disused railway bridge and keep on to reach a park beside the road bridge at Stamford Bridge. Go through this and then right along Main Street back to the start.

Points of interest

Stamford Bridge – Close by is the site of the battle fought in 1066 in which King Harold defeated Harald and his Viking army, perhaps leaving him a little weaker to fight at Hastings.

WALK

88 Pocklington

START At SE8034905, Pocklington,
YO42 2AB

DISTANCE 7 miles (11.3 km)

SUMMARY A moderate walk mainly
on field and woodland paths

PARKING Pay and display car parks in
Pocklington

MAPS Explorer 294; OS Sheets
Landranger 106

WHERE TO EAT AND DRINK Various
places to eat and drink in
Pocklington

A pleasant walk on the edge of the Wolds.

1 Head north-east along Market Place (the B1246). Keep right,
at The Feathers Hotel, onto Union Street. Follow this. At the end,
keep right onto London Street. Keep along this until Target Lane is
reached, go left onto this, keeping left onto a path between houses.
Follow this, cross over Denison Road, and keep ahead, climbing
Chapel Hill Road. At the top, cross the field into the woods, and
follow the path along the edge of the golf course. At the end of this,
the path descends through the trees. To join Woodhouse Lane, go left
along this to The Mile.

2 Go right along the road until a footpath sign on the right. Cross
over the stile and cross the field, aiming for Mill Farm in the distance.
Pass to the left of the farm, then right along a track, leaving this by
going left into woods in front of the farm. A track follows the edge
of woods over fields to reach Swineridge Lane. Go right along the
road and follow it to the junction of Martin Lane on the outskirts of
Millington village.

3 Keep left at the junction and follow the road. At the junction
opposite the church, go left past the it, then right at the next junction.
Walk down into the village, and then go left at the footpath sign. Keep
right where the road forks, pass a house and then climb steeply to join
a track. Go right along this, still climbing towards Warren Farm. At

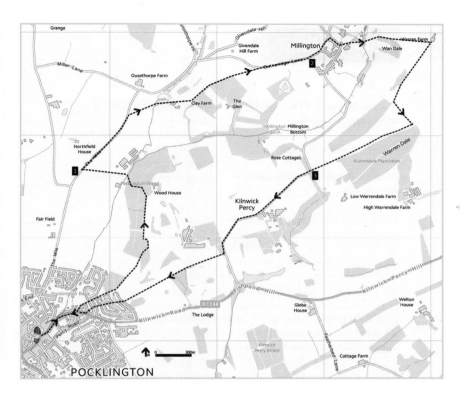

the fence on the top, go right along; there are good views back down to Millington below. Keep ahead towards the corner of a wood. Just before this, go left across the field to the corner of another wood. Go right along the edge of this wood and follow it downhill to a road.

4 Go straight ahead along a road, pass Kilnwick Percy village, and keep along the road until it turns at the corner of a wood. Just after this, go right over a fence onto the golf course. Follow the path over the course to emerge onto Gus Walker Drive. Go straight over and follow the path down between the houses to reach St Helen's Road. Go right, then left onto Chapel Hill Road. Follow this to a footpath on the right, go down this to Denison Road. Go left here to the B1246, and right along it to Target Lane, then retrace outward route back to the centre of the village.

89 Bracey Bridge

START At TA076619, Bracey Bridge picnic area, YO25 4DE

DISTANCE 7 miles (11.3 km)

SUMMARY A moderate walk mainly on field paths

PARKING Roadside parking

MAPS Explorer 295; OS Sheets Landranger 101

WHERE TO EAT AND DRINK None

A pleasant walk linking three historic villages.

1 From the picnic area, go through the kissing gate leading onto the access track to Bracey Bridge Mill. Follow this until just before the road. Here, bear left along a grassy track and follow it along the field edge until a facing hedge is reached.

2 Go diagonally left to join a track, go left along this and follow it to the road in Harpham. Go right and follow the road through the village to the crossroads.

3 Go left at these onto Butt Balk. Soon after go right onto a narrow path between houses. The path goes diagonally left over the field beyond, keep on in the same direction over several fields to reach the road in Burton Agnes village. Go right along this and walk through the village to the crossroads.

4 Go right at these, onto Station Road. Keep on along this, crossing the railway line, to a junction at the edge of trees. Go right along this road, Outgates, and follow it over fields. Re-cross the railway line and keep on back to Harpham village. Just before the crossroads, go left into a yard via a gate, cross the field beyond, and then along a narrow path to Daggets Lane. Go right along this to the junction with Cross Gates.

5 Go left and then right through the churchyard. Keep on over fields to reach Station Lane. Go left along this, to a gate on the right. Go through this to cross a stream. Keep ahead towards woods,

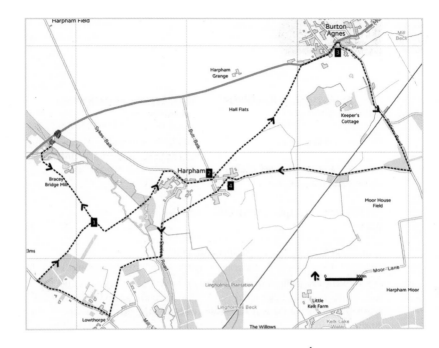

follow the right edge of this to its end. Go left along a track to Mill
Lane. Go right along this, and then right again at the next junction.
Follow this road, passing the church on your right, then at the far
end of Church Wood, go right onto a track. Follow this along the
edge of the woods, and then the field beyond back to the facing
hedge.

[6] Go left and follow the outward route back to the picnic area.

Points of interest

Harpham – The local squire was once St Quentin; his family were
said to be haunted by the ghost of a drummer boy drowned in the
well. There is an annual blessing service at St John's Well.

Driffield

Start At TA025577, Driffield, YO25 6LR

Distance 7 miles (11.3 km)

Summary A moderate walk mainly on field and riverside paths

Parking Pay and display car park in Driffield

Maps Explorer 295; OS Sheets Landranger 106

Where to eat and drink Various places to eat and drink in Driffield

A pleasant walk along the Driffield canal.

① Exit the car park onto East Gate South, go right along this and follow it to the end. Where the road stops, keep ahead and cross the footbridge over the railway line. Keep ahead to the junction with Anderson Street.

② Go right and follow the road to the start of the Driffield Canal. Go left onto Riverside after the old mill buildings, now apartments. Follow this along the canal, then past a couple of riverside houses. Keep ahead along a muddy path, squeezed between the canal and the River Hull. Keep on along the canalside until you reach a set of lock gates beside the road.

③ Cross the lock gates, then go right along a permissive path between the road and the canal towards Wansford. At Wansford Lock, cross the road and keep on till you cross a stream.

④ Leave the road and go left along the stream. Pass in front of a house, with the stream running underneath it. Keep alongside Nafferton Beck over fields. At the road, go right to cross the beck and then left into the fields and continue to follow the beck upstream. Keep on until the next road is reached. Here, go left over the bridge, then right to cross over the railway line. Keep alongside the beck until you reach a metal gate in the corner of the field. Here, leave the beck and aim diagonally left across the field towards the houses, to another gate.

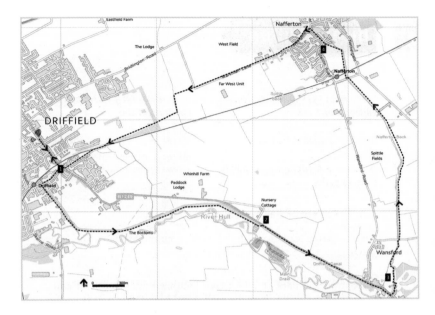

⑤ Go through this then right along the Priestgate, pass Nafferton Mere, then at the junction in front of the church go left onto Westgate. Follow this out of the village and keep on until it turns sharp right in front of a builder's yard. Leave the road and go into the field to the left of the buildings. Follow the track over the field to a ditch. Go left along this then right over a footbridge. Keep ahead to enter woods, follow the muddy track through these to the railway. Go left along this onto Meadow Lane, follow this to the junction with Wansford Road. Go right and then left onto Anderson Street.

⑥ Go right to cross the footbridge and walk back along East Gate South to the car park.

Points of interest

Nafferton – A prominent church and the village pond or 'mere' is surprisingly large. Goldeneye and other waterfowl can be seen there along with mallards and swans.

91 Bishop Wilton

START At SE797550, Bishop Wilton village, YO42 1RX

DISTANCE 7¼ miles (11.7 km)

SUMMARY A moderate walk mainly on field paths

PARKING Roadside parking

MAPS Explorer 300; OS Sheets Landranger 100

WHERE TO EAT AND DRINK The Fleece Inn www.thefleeceinn.info

An interesting walk through the Wolds countryside, with fine views.

1 Leave the village by walking south along the road, past the Fleece Inn. Continue along the road until a footpath sign on the left is reached. Leave the road and enter the field and climb steeply alongside the hedge. At the top go right along the hedge, go through a gate onto the other side of the hedge and keep right and follow this to the road at Great Givendale. Go left along the road to the T-junction.

2 At the junction go diagonally left onto a track through trees, pass behind a small church and keep along the track through Given Dale. Cross a stream, then climb alongside the edge of a wood. At the top, keep ahead to a hedge. Go left uphill through the field to join a road. Go left along this and follow it to a road junction.

3 Go left onto The Bence and follow this as far as some power lines, then cross the road. Go left here and follow these over the field towards a wood. Walk alongside this and then follow the path down into Deep Dale. At the bottom, keep right onto a track. Follow this through the trees to eventually reach Beacon Road.

4 Go straight over the road and follow the track downhill to the corner of Crow Wood. Go left along the edge of the wood. At

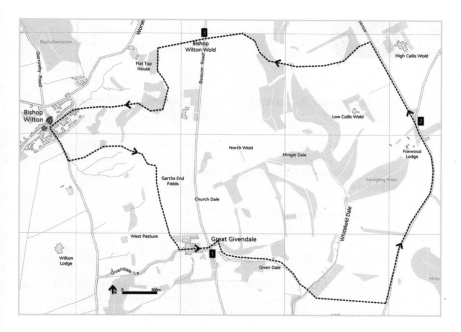

the far end, follow the fence contouring around the head of the
dry chalk valley. At the corner of the wood on the opposite side,
descend through rough pastures back to the village. Go left along
the road back to the start.

Points of interest

Bishop Wilton – A beautifully placed village just below the ridge
of the Wolds. The church spire is very prominent and a pleasant
stream runs through the village.

START At SE602521, York Minster,
YO1 7HH

DISTANCE 7½ miles (12 km)

SUMMARY A moderate walk mainly
on paved paths

PARKING Numerous pay and display
car parks in the city centre

MAPS Explorer 290; OS Sheets
Landranger 105

WHERE TO EAT AND DRINK Various
places to eat and drink in the city
centre

An interesting walk around the city and university campus.

① From the south-west corner of the minster, walk towards the small park on the corner of Duncombe Place, going left along this. Follow it to go left onto Lendal. Keep ahead to the junction at the B1227. Here, go left into Low Ousegate. Just before the bridge, go down steps on the left onto the riverside path. Go left and keep on along the riverbank to the confluence of the River Ouse and Foss. Cross the footbridge and keep on alongside the river. It's easy walking with fine views along the river. At the Millennium Bridge, keep left where the path forks, passing allotments. Keep ahead over open grassy area until the path makes a sharp left turn. Just after this, go right at the path junction, and pass some industrial units to join Love Lane. Keep straight on at the junction with St Oswald's Road, the path soon turns right back to the riverbank. Keep on to a bridge of a stream.

② Don't cross this, turn left and follow the stream. Cross another footbridge, keep ahead onto St Oswald's Court. Walk along this to Main Street, go right along here to where it forks. Go left along a path onto Germany Lane, keep on to the end of this, then keep ahead onto a track over fields. Follow this, bear right where it turns, then keep left at the next junction. Keep on over fields to just before the A64, go left over a field to enter the golf course. Go diagonally right over the course to join a track. Go left along this and follow along the edge of the course to the club house, onto the road.

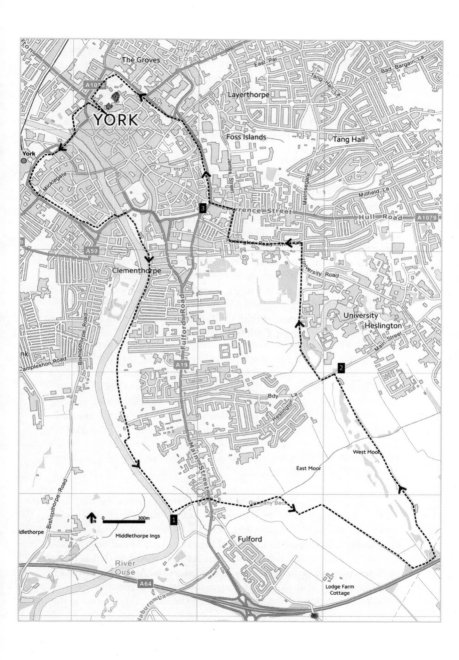

③ Go left along Heslington Lane, cross over and go right along the path leading into the grounds of York University. Keep left where it forks and follow it along the edge of the university grounds to University Road. Go left along this, keep on, then left into Thief Lane. Keep along this to the T-junction with the A19, Barbican Lane. Go right along this to the next T-junction, go right again and continue to Walmgate Bar, on your left. Go under the arch and climb up onto the city walls.

④ Go left along the walls to Red Tower, where the city walls end. Descend to street level and go left on Foss Islands Road, first past houses but soon to join the banks of the River Foss. There were never any walls built along this section as the city was protected by the river/marshes. Keep on to traffic lights, go left over the river, then cross over to the city wall on the other side of the road. Go left along the walls until you reach Monk Bar, descend to street level. Then climb the steep narrow stone stairs to the left of Monk Bar, and then go left along the city walls. There are grand views of the minster over the rooftops/gardens of the Treasurer's House. Keep on along the walls to reach Bootham Bar. Descend the stairs back down to street level again. Go left back to York Minster.

Points of interest

York has many points of interest in the city centre far too numerous to list here.

The Wolds Way

START At SE853742, Rillington, then get a bus to East Herlston to start the walk, YO17 8LH

DISTANCE 7½ miles (12 km)

SUMMARY A moderate walk mainly on field paths

PARKING Roadside parking

MAPS Explorer 301; OS Sheets Landranger 101

WHERE TO EAT AND DRINK The Coach and Horses
www.coachandhorsesrillington.com

A linear walk along the northern escarpment of the Yorkshire Wolds.

1 Leave the A64 and walk south along Church Lane, pass the church and go left along the lane leading out of the village. Follow this as it climbs up onto East Heslerton Brow towards Manor Wold Farm. Just before the farm, the corner of a wood is reached.

2 Go right here along the front of the trees, over fields. At the end of the second, the path goes left for a short distance then right. Keep on to reach another wooded area, go left along the front of it to a track. Go right along this to a road, cross this then go right along the edge of the field opposite. At the end of this field go left along its edge. Keep on over two fields to the corner of a wood. Go right into them and follow the track running along the edge of trees. Keep along this track until it makes a sharp right turn, downhill.

3 Leave the woods/track by going left, cross over another track and keep ahead along an old earthwork to reach more woods. Enter these. Where the track goes sharp left, keep straight ahead, downhill, to join another track. Go left along this and keep on. At the edge of the trees the track turns left. Shortly after this, it starts to bear left uphill. Go right here, exit the woods and cross a field to the corner of a road. Go right along a track over fields behind Winteringham village to a road. Go right along it and follow it to where it forks.

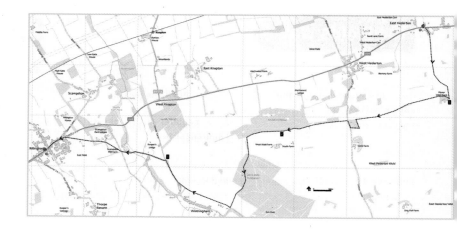

④ Take the left fork and follow the road to a T-junction. Go right a short distance, then go left over fields towards Fir Plantation. Cut through the corner of this and keep on over more fields to the A64. Go left along this into Rillington.

Points of interest

Yorkshire Wolds Way – A National Trail in Yorkshire that runs 79 miles from Hessle to Filey, around the Yorkshire Wolds. When at Filey Brigg, it joins with the Cleveland Way, another National Trail. In 2007, the Yorkshire Wolds Way celebrated the twenty-fifth anniversary of its official opening on 2 October 1982.

Hunmanby

Start At TA094775, Hunmanby village, YO14 0JT

Distance 7½ miles (12 km)

Summary A moderate walk mainly on field paths

Parking Roadside parking

Maps Explorer 301; OS Sheets Landranger 101

Where to eat and drink Various places to eat and drink in Hunmanby

A pleasant walk with fine views.

① Walk west along Malton Road. Follow this out of the village to the track on the left leading to Windmill House. Go left along this track and follow to Field House Farm. At the farm go left past the buildings along the field edge, then right behind them to a track leading left over fields. Take this and follow over fields to a T-junction.

② Go right along a track and descend into Stocking Dale. Go right along the valley bottom, keeping right where it forks. At the far end where it curves left, keep straight ahead, climbing to a field. Go along the right hand edge of this. At the far side go right and cross the field to a track. Keep on in the same direction along the track to reach the road at Stockendale Farm.

③ Cross the road onto a track, follow this over fields as far as overhead cables. Go right through the hedge, and cross diagonally across the field to the corner of a hedge. Go through this and then follow the left edge of the field. Keep on over several fields to reach Flotmanby Lane.

④ Go right along this and follow it into Muston village. Keep ahead through the village, ignore High Lane on the right, to reach a T-junction with the A165. Go right along this to the roundabout. Take the track on the south side of the roundabout and follow it over fields to North Moor Farm. Go left onto its access track and follow it back to the outskirts of Hunmanby. At the houses, keep right along Northgate, follow this round to the junction with Castle Hill. Go right back to the start.

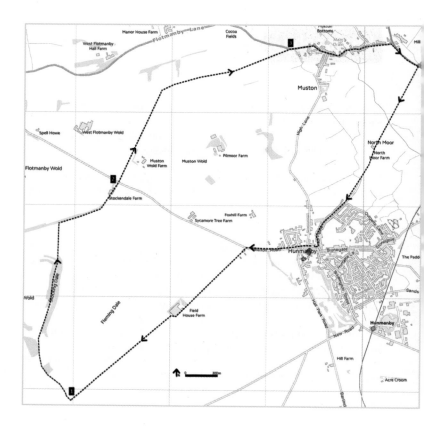

Points of interest

Hunmanby – The main market town for the East Riding of Yorkshire and the last place in England where King Stephen kept his wolfhounds. It has numerous important buildings, including Low Hall. The original hall was founded in the eleventh century, and Hunmanby Hall, a Stuart era building, was erected to replace the original hall on a more elevated site. The Hall was built from stones which were taken from Filey Brigg.

Wharram Percy

START At SE867644, Wharram Percy, YO17 9TN

DISTANCE 7¾ miles (12.5 km)

SUMMARY A moderate walk mainly on field paths

PARKING Medieval village car park

MAPS Explorer 300; OS Sheets Landranger 100

WHERE TO EAT AND DRINK None

A fine walk exploring the ridges and valleys between two Wolds villages.

① Take the track at the east side of the car park and follow it downhill. After passing through trees, the track curves around to the left to reach the site of the medieval village. Pass the ruins of the old church, cross the stream and climb left up the side of Deep Dale. The track now runs along the top edge of this, first south then curving around to the west. Deep Dale soon peters out, keep on over fields in the same direction to reach a track at a corner of a field.

② Don't go onto the track, turn left away from it, heading south to enter Vessey Pasture Dale. Where this opens out on both sides, keep straight ahead and climb the steep slope of Vessey Hill. At the top, cross over a field to join a track, go left along this. Keep on past Cow Wold Barn, then descend into Thixendale village. Go left to the church.

③ Keep on through the village, going left past the Cross Keys. At the end of the houses, keep on through fields along the bottom of Water Dale. Cross one track, and at the second, go left along it, then keep right where it forks. Leave the track shortly after this and climb right up the grassy slopes of Court Dale. Walk along the top edge of the valley. At the far end, a wooded area is reached, go right at the corner of these onto a track. Follow this over the field, then go right at the junction. Follow this track over fields till it enters woods and bears left.

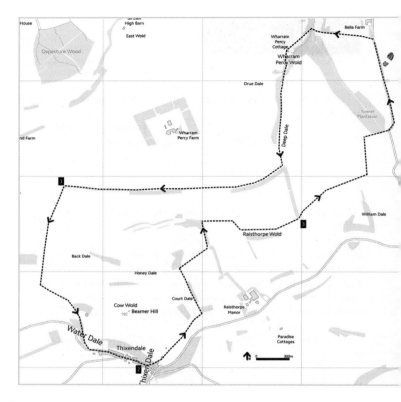

(4) Leave it and go right through trees into a field. Follow the left edge of the field round to woods, and go left along wide grassy path to another track. Go left along this, keep right at the end of the woods, and continue over two fields. Go left along the hedge/fence over fields to a track. Go right along this past woods to a road. Go left along this back to the car park.

Points of interest

Wharram Percy – The remains of the medieval village will provide lots of interest for those interested in archaeology.

Warter

START At SE871503, Warter village, YO42 1XR

DISTANCE 7¾ miles (12.5 km)

SUMMARY A moderate walk mainly on field paths

PARKING Roadside parking

MAPS Explorer 294; OS Sheets Landranger 106

WHERE TO EAT AND DRINK None

A fine walk through rolling Wolds countryside around Warter.

[1] From the centre of the village, walk east along the B1246. Keep left, passing the village church. Just after the pond, go left onto Mill Lane, opposite houses. Follow this uphill, keep left at the junction, and continue uphill until the road turns left. Leave it and go right along a track along the field edge. At the end of the field, go left and continue to the junction of tracks in the corner.

[2] Go right along the track and follow it over fields to Lavender Dale. Descend left into the valley bottom, and head north along it. Where it forks, keep right and climb to join a track. Go right along this, then left through a gap in the trees to Blanch Farm. Keep to the left of the buildings, then go right after them onto a track. Go right along it and follow over fields to a T-junction.

[3] Keep straight ahead on the track to reach the B1246, cross this to join a track in the field on your right. Follow this over fields, cross a lane at the corner of a wood. Keep ahead over fields on the track to the next woods. Turn right in front of them and follow them to join a road.

[4] Go left along the road and then go right onto a wide grassy track, follow this. It turns left before descending into Great Dug Dale. Walk through this, at the end join the B1246 again. Go left along this and walk back into Warter village.

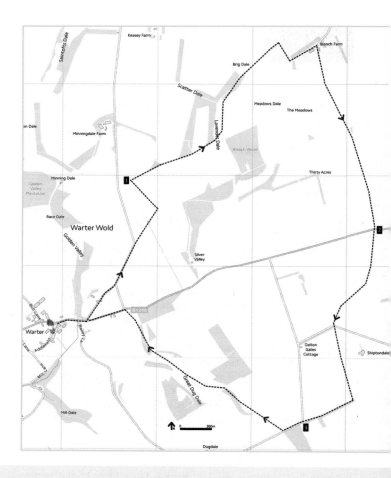

Points of interest

Warter – One of East Yorkshire's most attractive villages, located in the Yorkshire Wolds, around four miles from Pocklington. The village's church, St James, has recently been restored and is now open as a Heritage Centre. Nearby to Warter was one of David Hockney's most recent subjects, *Bigger Trees Near Warter*, which is part of the 2012 exhibition: A Bigger Picture.

Nether Poppleton

START At SE556549, Nether
Poppleton, YO26 6LL

MAPS Explorer 290; OS Sheets
Landranger 105

DISTANCE 8¼ miles (13.3 km)

WHERE TO EAT AND DRINK Various
places to eat and drink in Nether
Poppleton

SUMMARY A moderate walk mainly
on field and riverside paths

PARKING Roadside parking

A fine walk along the banks of the River Ouse.

[1] Follow the footpath from Main Street over the fields to New
Farm. Pass to the right of this and then go left behind the buildings
over fields to Lords Lane.

[2] Go right along this to Woodhouse Farm. Just before it, go left
to cross the Foss. Keep on to some buildings, go along the track in
front of these. At the field corner, go left to Thickpenny Farm. Keep
to the left of the buildings along a track, which then bears left away
from the farm. Keep along this to a T-junction.

[3] Go right and follow this to Park Farm. Pass this and shortly
afterwards, the road turns right in front of trees. Stay on the road,
following the edge of the woods. Where it turns sharp right away
from them, leave it and go left into Redhouse Woods. Follow the
track through these. At the other side, go right for a short distance
then left and follow the edge of the field around to join a road. Go
right along this. Where it turns right, leave it and keep on in the
same direction over a field, passing behind houses to reach the
banks of the River Ouse.

[4] Go right and follow the banks of the river back to Nether
Poppleton. It is about 4 miles of easy walking with grand riverside
views.

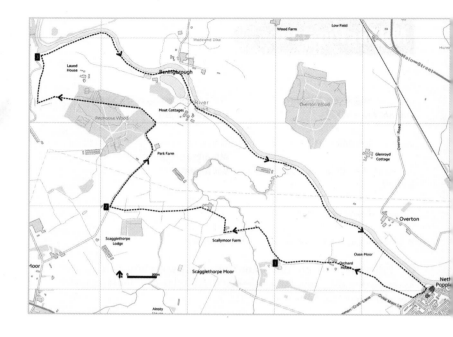

Points of interest

River Ouse – Navigable along its length, with the help of locks.
A few boats are moored along its banks, and others are likely to
provide interest as they pass by.

Millington Dale

START At SE831518, Millington village, YO42 1TX

DISTANCE 8¼ miles (13.3 km)

SUMMARY A challenging walk mainly on field paths

PARKING Roadside parking

MAPS Explorer 300; OS Sheets Landranger 100

WHERE TO EAT AND DRINK The Gait Inn, Millington
www.gait-inn-millington.co.uk

A lovely walk through steep sided Wolds valleys.

1 Leave the village by walking up Church Lane. At the top go right past the church along Swineridge Lane. At the next junction, keep left onto The Balk and follow this uphill. At the top, cross over the road and follow the track leading to Little Givendale Farm. Pass in front of the farm, and keep straight ahead onto a grassy track on the left edge of the field, to the far corner.

2 Go right along the hedge and follow it uphill to join a road. Go left along this and follow it to the track leading to Millington Heights. Go right along the track, which passes to the right of the farm. Keep on over fields. Where it forks, keep left along the field edge and descend to join the road in Millington Dale.

3 Go left along the road and follow it through the valley bottom to where Millington Dale forks into Frendal Dale and Pasture Dale. Leave the road and go right through a kissing gate and climb steeply for a short distance. The path levels off to reach a gate, go through this and descend into Nettle Dale. Go right through the gate then left onto a track. Follow this, keep left where it forks and keep on to descend into Sylvan Dale. Where the track turns sharp right in the bottom, leave it and go diagonally left uphill past the edge of woods. Keep climbing alongside a fence. Where this turns right, follow it, now across fields to Warren Farm.

(4) The path turns right, then almost immediately left along the field edge, to pass in front of the buildings. Keep along the field edge, until just before the corner of a wood. Go left over fields to the corner of a wood to your left. At the corner go right along the edge of the trees and follow it downhill to a road. Go right along the road and follow it back into Millington village.

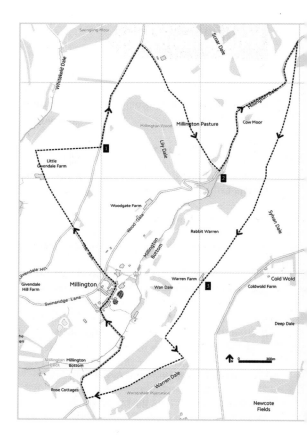

Points of interest

Millington – One of the Wolds' most attractive villages, it contains many old cottages and farms which shelter under the steep slopes of the Wolds.

Garrowby

Start At SE797550, Bishop Wilton village, YO42 1RX

Distance 8¾ miles (14 km)

Summary A difficult walk mainly on field paths with some road walking

Parking Roadside parking

Maps Explorer 300; OS Sheets Landranger 100

Where to eat and drink The Fleece Inn
www.thefleeceinn.info

An interesting walk through the Wolds countryside, with fine views.

1 Go north along Garrowby Road, then left into Vicarage Lane. Follow this, along the backs of gardens to Thorny Lane. Go right along this to the T-junction, then left along Bray Gate. Keep along this to a footpath sign on the right, beside a telegraph pole. Go right across fields and follow the path to Awnhams Beck. Go left along this to a road. Go right along the road till a left turn, leave it and cross fields towards woods. Just before these, go right over the field to Awnhams Beck again. Go left along this to the road.

2 Cross the road onto Barf Lane, follow this till it bends to the left. Leave it and go right over three fields. Then go left over one field, before going right again. Follow the left edge of the field around to a bridge over a stream. Cross this and head to the farm, follow its access track to Bugthorpe Lane.

3 Go right along the lane and follow it to just after Pasture Farm. Leave it and go right over fields, passing Glebe Farm to Kirby Underdale.

4 Go right, heading south along Water Lane. Keep along this as it climbs up onto Garrowby Wold, to a junction with the A166. Cross over this onto Worsendale Road, then keep left as the road descends to follow the track along the top of the wooded valley. Keep on to reach Crow Wood. Go left along the edge of the wood. At the far end,

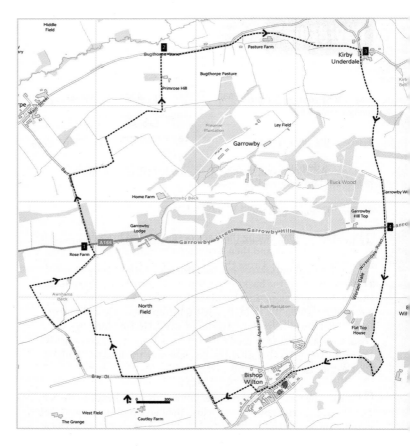

follow the fence contouring around the head of the dry chalk valley. At the corner of the wood on the opposite side, descend through rough pastures back to the village. Go left along the road back to the start.

Points of interest

Bishop Wilton – A beautifully placed village just below the ridge of the Wolds. The church spire is very prominent and a pleasant stream runs through the village.

Winteringham

START At SE879733, Winteringham village, YO17 8HU

DISTANCE 10 miles (16 km)

SUMMARY A demanding walk mainly on field and woodland paths

PARKING Roadside parking

MAPS Explorer 300; OS Sheets Landranger 100

WHERE TO EAT AND DRINK None

A walk through steep sided Wolds valleys with fine views.

① Leave the village along the track beside the red brick house, cross Winteringham Beck and then go diagonally right across the field to the corner of a hedge. Cross this then go right along the path to a cross track.

② Go right then almost immediately left onto a track along a field edge. Follow this over fields, past a pond to Thorpe Bassett. Go left and walk through the village, keeping left where the road forks, onto Water Lane. Follow this to a footpath sign on the right, leave the road and follow the path over fields, alongside a stream. Keep on in the same direction to the corner of a wood, descend alongside this, and then across fields to a road.

③ Go along the track to Wold House. Just before then, buildings descend steeply to the right. Follow a stream, past a pond, then climb right to the edge of woods. Go left along the edge of the trees. Go through a gap in the trees to join a track, then go left along this to a road. Go left downhill to the next track on the left.

④ Keep on downhill, pass a lake on your left, then at the T-junction go right. Walk along the road to the next T-junction. Here, go right into the village. Cross the stream and then go right at the T-junction and follow the lane along the back of the houses. Pass the church to reach the road near the lake. Go left back to Horse Course Lane.

⑤ Go right along the track and follow it to Low Bellmanear. Go

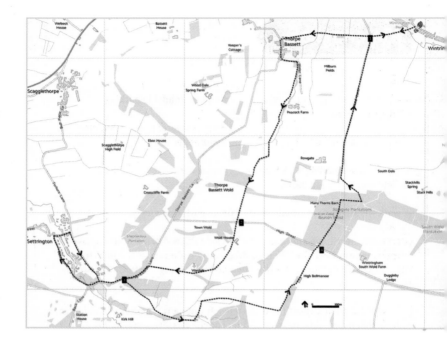

left here and follow the track as it climbs Fizgig Hill. Pass the edge of woodlands, and keep on uphill to a track junction on the edge of more woods. Go left along this and follow it past High Bellmanear to a road.

6 Cross the road and take the track ahead, which leads down through woods. It makes a right turn, then at the next junction, keep left to descend steeply. At the bottom go right at the junction, pass a pond and the entrance to Rowgate. Keep along the track to reach Kold Lane.

7 Go right and retrace outward route back to the village.